Jug Fishing for Greazy

and other Brad Paisley Fishing Stories

By Brad Paisley
and
M.B. Roberts

Rutledge Hill Press™
Nashville, Tennessee

A Division of Thomas Nelson Publishers, Inc.
www.ThomasNelson.com

This book is dedicated to my dad and my grandfather, Doug Paisley and Warren L. Jarvis. My best memories from my childhood are of the three of us fishing on the Ohio River. Thanks for taking me, teaching me how, and some of the best times of my life.

Published by Rutledge Hill Press, a Division of Thomas Nelson, Inc., P.O. Box 141000, Nashville, Tennessee, 37214.

Enhanced CD accompanying this book contains "I'm Gonna Miss Her" written by Brad Paisley and Frank Rogers. © 1999, 2001 EMI APRIL MUSIC, INC. and SEA GAYLE MUSIC. All RIGHTS Controlled and Administered BY EMI APRIL MUSIC, INC. (ASCAP). All Rights Reserved. International Copyrights Secured. Used by Permission.

Library of Congress Cataloging-in-Publication Data

Paisley, Brad.
    Jug fishing for Greazy and other Brad Paisley fishing stories / by M. B. Roberts.
      p. cm.
    ISBN 1-4016-0081-6 (hardcover)
    1. Fishing—Anecdotes. 2. Fishing—Humor. 3. Fishing stories. 4. Paisley, Brad. I. Roberts, M. B. (Mary Beth) II. Title.
SH441 .P25 2003
799.1—dc21   2002152043

Printed in the United States of America

03 04 05 06 07—5 4 3 2 1

Contents

Foreword

With Brad Paisley, fishing is number one. He's got his priorities straight. I like that.

One of the main ingredients to being a great fisherman is to love it. And Brad does. He absolutely loves it. You can tell, because when he's fishing, he's intense,; he's concentrating, and he loves landing fish. He really lights up when he catches one. He's got a passion for the sport. Plus, he really is a dang good fisherman.

It wouldn't take him long before he'd be out on the pro circuit. He's got all the ingredients. You can tell he's done it a lot as a kid. He understands water and techniques. It takes a lot of practice. But as far as reading the water and knowing where to cast and knowing where you should be positioned, he's right there. He knows all that stuff.

Brad and I first met about two years ago. We finally got together to go fishing and film an episode for my show in September of 2001. We caught a lot of fish that day and just had a terrific time. From the start,

I gave him a hard time, and he gave me a hard time. Brad can be so serious that it's hard to get the ice broken if you don't cut up right away. So that's what we did. He'd get on me about being old, and I'd tell him that he can't sing as good as I do.

Well, Brad really is a good prankster, and he does it in a sneaky way. About a month after the show, we met up at Tthe Kentucky Speedway where my son, Hank Parker, Jr., was racing in a Busch race. Brad was playing, and he had about forty thousand40,000 people out there wadded up listening to him and having a big time. So, I waited till he was through and then went backstage to see him. I wanted him to meet my wife, Martha. Well, Brad came over, but the crowd kept clapping. so hHe had to go back onstage and do an encore. He said, ""C'mon!""

I said, "tThere is no way!"

He said, ""No, C'mon! C'mon! I just want to introduce you.""

So I get on stage with him and he starts singing, "I'm Gonna Miss Her" (Tthe Fishin' Song), and of course he's not gonna shut up until I sing. And I can't sing a lick! So there'res 40,000 forty thousand people screaming for me to sing. So I sang. And it was bad.

I told him I was going to pay him back by editing the show we did, which had not aired yet, so all the viewers would see was him picking out a backlash the whole time. I'd be catching fish like crazy, and we'd keep cutting to Brad just sitting in the back picking out a backlash.

I still might have done that, but Brad saved himself by asking me to be in his video for "I'm Gonna Miss Her." That song is a killer! It's just great.

I think I'm more famous for this being in the video than anything else! A few years ago I did a McDonald's commercial, and I thought after I'd done that I had arrived. But it took being in the Brad Paisley video to truly arrive!

That day was a lot of fun. We got some fishing in for sure. Brad likes to fish so much that he didn't want to miss out. We were on a great lake that belongs to a friend of mine in the middle of the country, about an hour and a half south of Montgomery, Alabama. The fishing was great. We went out for a couple of hours, then we got serious. Boy, Brad had his game face on that day. I laughed at him all day. He was real serious. He was on top of everything.

I still get comments about the video all the time. People laugh at me and say, ""You were really sawing on the guitar, and you don't know what you're doing, do ya?""

That's probably the only stab I'll make at music. I can't even play the radio. It's good to know your weaknesses. There are three kinds of people: people who know, people who don't know, and people who don't know they don't know. At least I know I don't know!

So, I'll leave the music making to Brad. And fish with him whenever I get the chance!

Hank Parker
September 2002

Acknowledgments

The authors would like to thank the following people for making this book possible:

Hank Parker, Jimmy Houston (and the folks in their offices!), Forrest Wood, Doug and Sandy Paisley, Nancy Wade, Cindy Bartsch, Frank Rogers, Kelley Lovelace, Tim Owens, Peter Zavadil, Hank Parker, Jr., Jerry Springer, Tracy Byrd, Andy Griggs, Darryl Worley, Little Jimmy Dickens, Dawn Wells, Richard Stanczyk, Joe Bucher, Fred Telleen, Barry Dodson, Goose Gossage Kent Hrbek and Ron Modra.

A special thanks to all the folks on Brad's team especially Jimmy Gilmer, Allen Brown, Leslie Paulin, Susan Sherrill, Brent Long and Kris Marcy.

Introduction

Like my friend Jimmy Houston says, the cool thing about fishing is it doesn't matter if it's the governor, the president, or a famous actor (or singer)—when they get out in the boat, they're just guys or girls liking to fish. It's like an instant friendship.

In the meet-and-greet lines it seems like all my fans want to talk about is fishing. I guess they must have heard I'm into it. I get more fishing gifts than anything else. They give me inspirational things based on fishing: carved wooden trinkets that read "Teach me to Fish and I Fish for a Lifetime," antique baits, and little fisherman statues. I could decorate my house with the things they give me. In fact, I have decorated my house with all this great stuff! I even have a full-sized, flat-bottomed boat hanging on my wall that my friend, songwriter Tim Owens, made for me!

Almost every day I hear a fishing story from somebody! To put it simply, fishing is a metaphor for life. With bass fishing especially, you've got to be ready to change whatever tactics you had in mind. You get out there and realize that it's not the day you thought it'd be. Maybe it's overcast, and you thought it would be sunny; or maybe the water is muddier than you'd planned. Just like life in general, you always have to be ready to improvise.

One of my favorite charities is Teach a Child to Fish. When you take a kid fishing, you instantly teach him things he's going to need to know when he gets older, like adaptation and patience. Patience is a big thing when it comes to fishing. You've got to be patient. I don't know any situation in life where you get the luxury of being impatient. I've heard people say they don't like to fish because it's just too boring. It takes too long. But you know what? They've got a lot to learn yet.

When I was a kid, I looked forward to going fishing more than anything else. It was the coolest thing that we could do. If I knew we were going fishing one weekend, it was hard to sleep the night before.

The earliest fishing memory I have is sitting in a boat with my grandfather and my dad. You know how when you get older your earlobes hang down and kind of droop? Well, my grandfather's earlobes were flapping in the wind as we went down the river. My dad and I were laughing at him because of that. It's one of those great memories of everybody just cracking up about something totally bizarre. I guess it's not always about how many fish you catch.

But seriously, it seemed like out on the water we would talk less but would bond more. When you're on the boat, your mind is only on fishing. It's a cleansing time. You think of nothing for a while. It's similar to yoga in that the trick is to clear your mind.

Out on the lake, guys who are fishing don't really think about—at least I don't—the bills you need to pay or the speeding ticket you just got or even problems in a relationship. You just sit and try to figure out what's going to make a big, fat bass hit a lure. You can go out with no heads-up at all about what somebody's really like. Then after a day on the water, you feel like you know them so much better. You really form a bond.

Mostly, fishing takes down people's guard. It's very primal. It's a man and a fish and you're trying to catch it. You don't have to have any sort of pretense. It's about practicality. You're working side by side with somebody. It's not really a competition. You find yourself part of a team, working on the common goal of seeing how many fish you can catch. For me, it just makes sense. I love fishing.

—Brad Paisley

On Bass, 24/7

All fishermen are not alike. Even though they have the sport itself in common, anglers split into passionate camps when it comes to the fish they pursue. Some fishermen will only go after deep-sea trophies, such as blue marlin found off the coast of Mexico. Some fishermen spend a lifetime casting for the elusive musky in the northern lakes of Canada. Some guys will only cast for trout with hand-tied flies. Then there are bass fishermen—a breed unto themselves.

B ass fishing is my favorite. I believe it's the most challenging kind of fishing. Bass are magnificent fish, and I'm always thinking about catching that really big one. My friend Alan Jackson feels the same way. In fact, we've talked about going down to Mexico to get one of the monsters down there.

Here in Tennessee, the chances of catching a large fish are slim because the bass are all the same size. It's rare to find giants where I live. But they're in there, and you know it. That's part of the challenge.

Brad Paisley fishing in Branson, Missouri

I don't really eat bass. I have in the past from waterways where it's necessary. For instance, I've kept and eaten fish out of a pond where there are too many. But most of the time, it's all about the sport. I'll catch the thing, and it'll go right back in.

To catch bass, you've got to have a special boat, and you have to know something about bass fishing. You can't just go catch a bass blindly. Well, you could get lucky certain times of the year—bass can be caught all year long with the right equipment and knowledge. But mostly, it's just like learning anything. You have to study it a bit.

In the summertime, the best time to go fishing is after dark. There are certain hours of the night when it's good. Right at dark it's not that great, but between one and three in the morning, then again at dawn, that's when it's really good. It all depends on how late you are willing to stay out. When I went fishing with Hank Parker for his show, we weren't off that boat more than an hour or two. More than once I've fished from sundown one day to sundown the next!

Even after a marathon like that, my legs don't get too stiff because I know nice little places you can get out and eat. When we're at my friend Kelley's pond, his mother-in-law fixes the best food—mashed potatoes, creamed corn, okra, and pork chops. They live right on the property. So we fish all day, go up and eat lunch, go out again, and come back to find dinner ready. Then we go back out until dark, go in, and go to sleep—and do it all again the next day.

My dad says I'm the guy who won't go in. The last time we went fishing, I kept him out on Percy Priest Lake in Nashville a lot longer than he would have liked. It started to rain and the sky got a little black—

OK, there was some lightning—but I just didn't see any reason to pack it in. Everybody knows the rain can help get the fish biting. As long as it's warm enough, you're OK. If it's above fifty degrees and raining, I don't care! I'll put on a raincoat. That'll do.

Brad fishing with a guide (center) and his dad (right) in Branson, Missouri

My record for staying out fishing is probably fourteen hours. Those are the times I've slept on my boat on Percy Priest Lake. I've launched and then gone and found an island or anchored in a cove and just slept out there after night fishing. It makes perfect sense. You go out fishing in the evening before nightfall. When it gets dark, you go anchor. Later, you go to sleep. Then at dawn, you wake up, fish a little bit, and go home.

Last year, I spent my birthday, October 28, out on the lake by myself. I stayed all night. When I launched, it was going on 8:00 P.M., so it was already dark. I fished awhile, then I drove across the lake and found a cove, anchored there, and went to sleep. With the coyotes!

Being out there is really incredible. At night, when you're on that boat and you've anchored and been there for a while, you sort of become part of things, and the animals forget about you. The lake acts a whole lot differently when it forgets that you're there. You can pull up in your boat, turn off the motor, stand there for a little bit, and it's deathly quiet. But once you're there for about thirty minutes, things start to happen. Things splash and make noise. Coyotes run along the bank in the middle of the night.

On my birthday, I was anchored right there in the middle of the lake. There was a full moon, and I could see everything. It was safe because it was a really calm evening. No chance of rain. It wasn't that cold. I have a really good sleeping bag, one that will handle up to thirty degrees below zero. But that night it only got down to around forty-five degrees.

Sometimes when I night fish, I throw my sleeping bag in the boat just in case. But that time I brought it on purpose. I planned to stay out all night. One of the nice things about my bass boat is that it has a really nice deck up front that's about eight feet wide. It's perfect for sleeping.

Come to think of it, I didn't sleep very well that night. But that really wasn't the point. A night like that is really the way to get inside yourself and think. It's definitely not the life I'm used to right now. Serious quiet is hard to find. I don't think I thought about anything important, really. And I only caught one or two fish the next morning. But that wasn't really the point either. It was just the right way to celebrate my birthday.

Jug Fishing for Greazy

There are fish and then there are legends. What is it about the one that won't be caught? The proverbial one that got away? Every time an angler tells the story, the legend grows—along with a fisherman's determination to finally one day scoop it into his net.

Kelley Lovelace, my friend and songwriting partner, has taken me on some great trips to Sand Mountain, Alabama, where his wife's parents live. Before we went up there the first time, Kelley told me all about the hybrid catfish that live in the two-acre pond on their land. He said there were only seven in the whole pond. Kelley's father-in-law, Dub, told him he knew there were only seven because since they were hybrids, they couldn't reproduce. Evidently, these fish were just huge. We decided there was only one thing to do: bring out the jugs.

We planned to spend the whole weekend fishing, so we came prepared. We brought milk jugs, water jugs, and a couple of two-liter Pepsi bottles too. The idea was to take the jugs, run lines down from them, and put chicken liver on hooks for bait. Then, if one of those huge fish tried to take the liver, it would set the hook on itself because it wouldn't be able to pull the jug down under the water.

So we got up at daybreak and loaded up Kelley's in-laws' little John boat. Then we motored out and set up our jugs on one end of the pond. We figured it might take a while for something to hit one of the jugs, so we decided to drive to the other end of the pond to fish for bass.

I ran the trolling motor. It didn't go very fast, so we took our time making our way to the other side of the pond. We found a place to stop, got set up, and started fishing. Well, it couldn't have been longer than ten minutes before we heard this huge splash. I turned and saw one of the jugs popping back up after it had been pulled way down under the water.

I looked over at Kelley and whispered, "Did you see that?" He said that my eyes were as big as saucers. Then I started hollering at him to reel in. We reeled in, and I took off toward the jugs. I was giving it all I had, but this little trolling motor could only go so fast. Man, we thought we had Moby Dick, or at least the Loch Ness monster on our hands. There was no way to tell.

We finally reached the spot where we saw the splash. I moved the boat around so Kelley could lean out and pick up the jug to see what was there. But as soon as we got close, that jug started moving. It looked like it was running from us.

I started moving the boat after him. The fish was definitely running from us. Kelley still couldn't reach it. He was yelling, "Give it all you've got!" Finally, we got ahead of it, and Kelley reached down and pulled the jug out of the water. At the end of it was at least a twenty-pound catfish. It was twenty pounds if it was an ounce! It was almost scary looking, like a nuclear fish or something.

Well, after we had a look at that greazy ol' thing (that's what we named him, Greazy), we put him back. We weren't going to eat him or anything.

All day, we caught those huge catfish. We know we got all seven of them, some of them twice, because we could tell where the hooks went in the first time. When we thought we'd caught all the catfish, we switched gears and went back to fishing for bass. It was probably the best day we ever had. We caught a ton, including one largemouth that I kept—a six and three-quarter pounder that pulled the boat!

I had that one mounted. Every time I look at it, I think of that great trip! But now, after hearing a story from Kelley, I'm dying to go back. Not long ago, Kelley went back to the pond with his brother and his friend Jeff Wood. Jeff was fishing with a little Zebco reel. After a couple of hours out there, Jeff got something. Something big. He worked the fish in close to the boat, and they all saw how big the fish was—a bass so big it looked like he was moving in slow motion. Anyway, they said it had to be between twelve and fourteen pounds. Twice as big as the one I got!

Anyway, the fish came up one more time, let all the guys look at him, then he dove straight down and took Jeff's reel all the way to the water. His line just snapped! He stood there silent for a while then started saying things Kelley was glad no one could hear.

The thing is, that fish, the big bass, is uncaught. Kelley and I agreed. If we don't get him by the time we're sixty-five or seventy, we're going to drain the pond!

Not everybody feels the same way Kelley and I do about catfish. Goose Gossage, the legendary relief pitcher with the signature mustache who played (most notably) for the New York Yankees, is one of those people.

Goose is a huge country music fan, by the way. He also loves to fish. He grew up trout fishing in Colorado at his family's fish camp. He has had some awesome times there. His father taught him to fish, and he in turn taught his three sons to fish. He said he has to admit that his fondest memories are probably with his dad. "When you've got three young sons, you spend all your time de-tangling lines and baiting hooks—for them! It's hard to get a line in yourself!"

But back in 1970, way before he became a dad, Goose was just starting out as a baseball player. He was on his way to becoming a player for the

Goose Gossage in Canyon City, Colorado

Chicago White Sox, but first he had to make a trip to a tiny town in Florida where he was a top prospect in the instructional league.

The aspiring players worked really hard down there, but they did manage to get a little bit of time off. Some of Goose's fellow players invited him to go catfishing. Goose was excited. He'd never even seen a catfish before.

They weren't out on the hot, swampy river for long when Goose landed his first catfish. He reeled it in and swung it into the boat where the fish began flopping around like crazy. Goose lifted his foot to step on the fish, and before the guys could stop him, he stomped down hard.

Well, nobody told the guy from Colorado that catfish have a big, sharp bone in their dorsal fin. It punctured Goose's shoe and pierced his foot. He wasn't hurt bad, but he hooted and hollered loud enough for them to hear him up in Chicago.

Goose says if he ever catches another catfish he will immediately cut the line. But Goose has never laid his eyes on Greazy. . . .

One more thing about catfish . . . I overheard Forrest Wood, the founder of Ranger Boats and my good friend, telling this story about a trip we took together:

Once when I was working in Kansas City my old buddy, Brad Paisley, came to visit me so I could show him a thing or two about fishing. On our way to my favorite fishing hole a man I didn't know stopped to share an interesting story. He said that he was fishing in the Missouri River and had put out some limb lines. When he came back a couple of days later to check them, the river had dropped, and his bait was out of the water about eighteen inches in places. When he looked under one of the limbs, he saw a catfish 'wringing wet with sweat' trying to get to his bait. We continued on and while we were on the river we came up on a man who was holding the boat steady in the current with a pole, and we asked him what he was doing. He said his brother was down under the water 'noodling' catfish. We asked him how long his brother normally stayed under. He replied, "If he takes his lunch, he stays all day!"

The Other Hank

World Champion bass angler Hank Parker is to fishing what Hank Williams is to country music. OK, some fishing aficionados, such as fans of Jimmy Houston or Bill Dance, might argue that point. But Hank Parker and his popular TV show, Hank Parker's Outdoor Magazine, *is undeniably one of the best-known and loved fishing shows. Hank's talent and know-how are legendary.*

Brad is among the many fishermen who religiously tune in to those weekend morning fishing shows. Even when he is on the road, after playing a late show, Brad will get up early and turn on the TV in his hotel room. Hank's show is one of the few things that could keep him off the lake—and away from his guitar.

I have always said that if I couldn't play music, I would want to host my own fishing show. OK, I'll admit it. I want to be Hank Parker. One of my earliest memories is of watching his show. I love reminding him of that, by the way. That it's one of my earliest memories. Shoot, I couldn't even drive yet, and he had already been on TV for how long? Anyway, Hank's been doing his show for going on twenty years.

Hank Parker, Brad Paisley, Doug Paisley, and Forrest Wood on the video shoot of "I'm Gonna Miss Her"

And he's more than just a great entertainer. He's earned the right to have a show. He's an awesome tournament fisherman. Hank was the first angler to win the Grand Slam of Bass Fishing, which includes the Classic, B.A.S.S. Angler of the Year, and the B.A.S.S. SuperBass Tournament. I do love watching his show.

I think my favorite episode is the one featuring Dale Earnhardt. It's funny, Hank told me that after all the shows he's taped, this episode sticks out as one of his favorites too. Dale and Hank were very close. They used to hunt and fish together. Anyway, Hank had asked Dale to come on the show, and Dale's daughter Taylor, who was about five at the time, and Hank's daughter Lucy, who was twelve, were on the show too.

So Lucy, Taylor, Dale, and Hank were fishing at the lake right behind Dale's house in North Carolina. Dale had some pretty big catfish in there, and right away, Taylor got one. She was fishing with a Mickey Mouse rod and reel and was having all kinds of trouble, so she just started walking backwards up the bank, dragging the thing instead of reeling it in. She just walked up the bank till it was out of the water! That killed me.

One afternoon Hank and I were talking about Dale Earnhardt as a driver. When he would have a misfortune on the race track, if he blew an engine or something like that, he wouldn't come in like many of the drivers do and give you an explanation as to what happened. If a guy like Dale Jarrett blew an engine, someone would ask, "Dale, what happened out there?" And Jarrett would say, "Well, I think we lost something in the valve train. We started losing oil pressure, and then later, we made a couple more laps and the whole engine just let go." If it was Earnhardt, they would question him, and of course he would know something broke in the valve train or something broke in the bottom, but he wouldn't explain that. When they would ask him what happened out there, he would just look up and say, "Blowed up!"

That was the end of the deal! Then he'd walk off.

So, back at the lake, Taylor had hooked another one. It was a big catfish that probably weighed twelve or fifteen pounds, and she was fighting that thing with her little Mickey Mouse rod and reel! Lucy was helping Taylor, but it was no use. Mickey just came apart. The fish broke the line, and the pieces went everywhere. Taylor sat there in disgust, looking at the little pieces of Mickey all over the ground. Earnhardt said, "Taylor, what happened?" She looked him dead in the face and said, "Blowed up!"

She didn't even think about it! I guess the apple doesn't fall far from the tree.

It was one of the biggest days of my life when I got to fish with Hank and be a guest on his show. It was a huge, huge thrill. I got some awesome stories too. I don't think we slept at all. It reminded me of Christmas. You don't want to go to bed because you're so excited, but you know if you don't, you're gonna be really tired. We fished all day and all night. Then got up at six the next morning and went again all day.

I was just in awe of him, but at the same time, he makes everyone around him feel so at ease. He is everything you'd think he'd be: funny and down to earth. We had a lot of fun kidding around. If he'd cast past the fish, I'd comfort him by saying it's just a near-sighted/far-sighted thing that comes with age. But really, Hank knows where the fish are without even looking. It's instinct with him. He's got the gift.

The man is as good a fisherman as he appears to be on his show. From the minute I climbed on his boat, I could tell he knew his stuff. Nothing can stump him. If there are fish in a lake, Hank will find them. We went out to a nine-hundred-acre private lake near Dothan, Alabama. We caught fish until we were tired of catching fish. Well, almost! We fished all day, then went out again at ten that night. I stayed out until I couldn't hold my eyes open anymore. We had to get up at six the next morning, and I was definitely the last one up. But fishing with him was awesome.

Of course, the whole time we were out I picked his brain and asked him all kinds of questions. We did a lot of talking. I learned about knots. He's a big fan of Palomar knots and ties almost everything on with it. I agree with him. He showed me a scale. Where a typical knot will break, this knot, the Palomar knot, is very effective. It retains something like 95 to 99 percent of the pound-test rating for a fishing line. I had already seen him do that on TV, but I was skeptical. But I found out it's true. He shared some other tips that day, too, like it's a myth that fishermen have to be totally quiet. As long as it's quiet under the boat you'll be OK. I guess for a guy who sings, this is a good thing to know. But Hank sings more than I do out there.

The best part of this whole experience was that Hank and I became good friends. A few weeks later I got him up on stage when I was playing a show at a Busch Race at Kentucky Motor Speedway. His son, Hank Parker Jr., is a driver, and Hank came to the show.

I walked off the stage before the encore and saw him standing there with his wife. I freaked! I said, "You've gotta come back up here." I brought him onstage, and we sang "I'm Gonna Miss Her." He's a terrible singer, but he acts like he's a good one on TV. After we sang he said, "Well you know, Brad actually caught more fish than me on the day I took him out, but when I edit that show, get ready. He'll be lucky if he gets more than a backlash."

Just wait. Someday I'll have my own fishing show, and I'll get him back.

Fathers & Sons

Ask any angler to tell a story about his father. Chances are, the story will involve the two of them at a pivotal moment in their lives. Likely, there won't be much talking. And they'll both have fishing poles in their hands.

When I meet people, even fellow country singers, if they love fishing like I do, that's what we'll end up talking about. It was that way when I met Andy Griggs. We'd already been friends for a few years when, in the fall of 2002, we ended up touring together on the CMT "Most Wanted Live Tour." All we ever talked about was when we were going to wet a line. We were always talking about trying to make it to a certain lake or that river, depending on where we were. We never seemed to talk about songs or the show!

Andy told me one of the most perfect fishing stories I've ever heard. It really sums things up for me. It involves him and his dad, who passed away a few years back.

Andy says when he thinks about the best times he had with his dad, it was when they were fishing. It was usually near their home in Monroe, Louisiana. They used to go pod fishing on the Ouachita River all the time when Andy was growing up. Then of course, when he got a record deal, there was less time for heading out to the river. But they did it when they could.

Not long before Andy's dad passed away, he went home for a visit. He says he could tell his dad had a lot on his mind. They hadn't been fishing for a while and Andy was dying to spend time with him. His dad was dying to spend time with Andy too. So this particular Saturday, even though it was raining really hard, they went anyway.

He says he won't ever forget sitting on the bank of that river. He was sitting Indian style next to his father. They had two lines in the water, and it was raining miserably.

Andy said, "Daddy, I don't think we're going to catch much fish in this weather." His dad had a real serious look on his face and answered: "That's all right son. It's not about the fish. Sometimes a man just needs to go fishing."

Andy says this was one of the coolest things he ever heard his father say. To this day, times come up when Andy tells his wife, "Ya know, I really just need to go fishing."

He says a lot of times he may not even carry a rod. Or he'll carry a rod and forget to even bait it up and throw it. He just gets so caught up in getting out there and getting his batteries recharged or getting things off his mind. I understand exactly what his dad was saying.

The first time I worked with the photographer Ron Modra, I walked in the room and he was talking with my manager, Jimmy Gilmer, about a fly-fishing trip he had just made down the Turnagain River in British Columbia. They talked much more about the trout he caught than what the heck we were supposed to be doing that day.

Ron grew up outside of Milwaukee, but he always considered Boulder Junction, Wisconsin, this little resort town way up north, as his home because every weekend he and his dad would blast up there to go fishing. His dad was a serious musky guy and spent every possible moment in search of his trophy fish. In fact, Ron's dad, Milt, was five hours away from home fishing for muskies the day Ron was born! Ron says that years later, when he found out his dad missed his debut into the world, he wasn't mad. He just asked him what he caught!

When I got to know him a little better, Ron shared a story about one particular fishing trip with his father. Ron was eighteen and had just graduated from high school. It was 1967, and he had also just been drafted into the army. He was on his way to Vietnam.

This is a little hard for me to imagine. I was three years old when the

Ron and Milt Modra in Boulder
Junction, Wisconsin

Vietnam War ended. But I think I might have dealt with a situation like this the same way.

By the time Ron finished basic training, then advanced-infantry training, it was early November. He came home to Milwaukee for two weeks' leave before he would be shipped off to Vietnam. With only a week or so left before he had to go, he and his parents had some pretty serious discussions about the possibility that he might not be coming back. There were a lot of tears. Then his dad asked him what he wanted to do with his last couple of days at home. He said he wanted to go to Boulder Junction.

So, Ron, Milt, and Milt's best friend headed up north. They went to the campground where they kept their camper and moved it over to their favorite lake. They were just in time. The guy who owns the campground was closing it for the winter. There was snow all over the ground. Things were freezing up. Technically, there was still one week left in Musky fishing season, but no one else was around!

They had the lake to themselves. They camped and fished for

muskies for five days. In a blizzard. No one caught a thing. And not much was said. Really, though, they spoke volumes.

Growing up in West Virginia, I went fishing with my dad a lot. But my grandfather, my mom's dad, was the one I fished with the most because he was retired. He had the time and always wanted to go. Whenever we could, the three of us went together. There was one time—I think I was twelve or so—that would be hard to forget.

Brad and Doug Paisley

My grandfather had cancer and was just starting to feel sick. My dad thought we should go fishing to get his mind off what had started to happen to him. So very early one morning, my dad, grandfather, and I took the boat and launched it at Moundsville, the next town over from Glen Dale, where we lived.

We went really early to beat the heat, but the problem was, the fog was incredibly thick. We started up the river a little bit, trying to stay away from this rock embankment that always seemed to have bats flying around it. We inched our way forward, and it got really foggy. Dad got in real close to the shore where he could see. He inched out a little bit more so we would have room to cast along the bank.

It's so silent that time of the morning. You can barely hear the birds out there. We're casting and we hear this whoosh! It sounds like something hitting the waves. I look up, and out of nowhere there's this huge barge, like the ones that push coal on the rivers.

We were probably forty feet from shore. Luckily, the boat was already pointed toward shore. So Dad just hit the engine and gunned it! When he hit the throttle, it threw me backward. My grandfather got thrown backward too. If he hadn't grabbed the motor, he would have gone overboard. While we were moving in, the barge was moving out. It missed us by about ten feet.

I guess that got my grandfather's mind off his troubles! We laughed about it later, but it was scary, eerie even. Dad was petrified. He looked peaked the rest of the day.

I think, being a kid, I got over it really fast. Looking back, I know why. My dad was the one driving the boat. And I trusted him.

Like many of us, Tracy Byrd fishes a lot with his dad. The cool thing is, it was Tracy who really got his dad into fishing. When he was a kid, it was his grandmother, his mom's mom, who taught Tracy to love the outdoors. Then he got his dad hooked.

Inspired by Tracy, his recently retired dad now fishes almost every day.

This year he caught a nine-foot, eleven-inch and a ten-foot, sixteen-inch within two days of each other. Pretty impressive!

One spring not too long ago, Tracy and his dad were fishing on the Sam Rayburn Reservoir, not too far from Tracy's home in Beaumont, Texas. After several rainy weeks, the water was way, way up. They couldn't let any water out of the dam because it would flood homes along the river.

So they were fishing this high, high water, which was actually in this man's cow pasture. The water was six feet over his fence.

Right away, this old farmer comes out and starts hollering and cussing at Tracy and his dad, telling them they were on his property. They said, "Sir, your property is under water. It is now part of the Corps of Engineers' reservoir. Wherever the water level goes, people can go." But the man called the game warden. He came out and said to the farmer, "I'm sorry, sir. But they can fish wherever they want." So Tracy and his dad kept fishing. They had already been out for three days and were just wearing 'em out! Catching tons of fish.

Tracy tells another story from this same trip that tickles me to death. Before they left, he and his dad watched a fishing show where the host said that a fish will never bite twice in the same day, reasoning that if a fish gets a hook in its mouth, it just won't bite again.

Well, Tracy and his dad were fishing this fifteen-acre area all day. At one point, Tracy threw out a big, white blade spinnerbait and dragged it through a hole when, bam! He had a big fish, about eight pounds. He reeled her in and got her next to the boat. The fish was hooked really well, so Tracy didn't think about his line being frayed or anything. He just kind of swung her into the boat instead of landing her with a net or lipping her. As he went to swing her into the boat, the line broke right at the knot, and she fell back in the water. He lost her. And she was just a hog!

So they kept fishing and Tracy's dad says, "Well, that guy said a fish won't bite twice. I guess that one's gone, then." About four hours later, they came back through the same spot. Tracy said, "Boy, it would be something if I could catch that big fish again." His dad reminded him that was impossible. That man on TV said they don't bite twice.

Tracy threw out a big eight-inch worm and got busy working along the area where he had hooked the big fish earlier when he felt a little bump, bump on his line. He set the hook and immediately the drag ran out. He said, "Dad, this may not be her, but it's another good fish!"

He reeled the fish in and got it next to the boat. He picked it up, and his dad says, "Well, I'll be danged." There was Tracy's white spinner bait hanging in her mouth! This time, he reached down and pulled her up by the lip.

He couldn't help himself. He grinned at his father and said, "Well, I guess lightning does strike twice!"

It's no surprise that Hank Parker Jr., the NASCAR driver, grew up fishing with his dad. His father, Hank Parker Sr., had been a pro tournament fisherman from before the time Hank Jr. was born. Junior's dad began starring on his own fishing show when Junior was only nine years old! He remembers when his dad taped that very first show. He and his brothers went out with him. That was a blast for young Hank.

He grew up absorbing pearls of wisdom from his fishing father. One saying popular around their house was: "Anything above 50 percent embellishment is a lie. Anything below 50 percent is OK."

One day of fishing really sticks out in Junior's mind. He went with his father to pre-fish before the Bass Masters Classic on the James River in Virginia. This time, they went out on Kentucky Lake. He remembers his dad planning the day.

Hank Sr. took out a map and said, "You know, the way this island is, we should really catch some fish. Let's try that out." They caught fish all day long. Big, five-pound fish. So many that Junior had to stop. His arm was too tired.

Hank Jr. says that was the point when he looked at his father with new respect. He realized that day that his dad was really gifted. Maybe before he thought he was good just because he looked up to him as his dad. After that day, he says he knew without a doubt—this guy is a great fisherman.

Everybody, including Hank Jr., thought he might grow up to be a pro fisherman too. It wasn't far-fetched to think he might even take over for his father some day. He has talent, is a great teacher, and he loves to fish.

But then he discovered racing. He describes himself as very competitive, and that fits with the sport. When he got into driving, he realized that he loved fishing, but it was something he did to escape and relax. As a NASCAR driver, it's more important than ever for him to have a way to be close to nature and not listen to a lot of noise. Plus, he says, he and his brother can go out on the boat and just sit there and troll. You won't see his dad doing that.

When my friend Kelley Lovelace married his wife, Karen, a few years back, he became a stepfather to Karen's little boy, McCain. Obviously, it was a huge event in his life. One night after they had gotten married and Kelley had settled into his role as stepfather and husband, we were sitting around trying to write a song. We were fresh out of ideas so I said to him, "Let's write something about you guys. Why don't we write something to make Karen cry?"

So that's what we did. That night, we wrote a song about step-fathers—the good ones—called "He Didn't Have to Be." It was right from the heart, talking about Kelley and this little boy he had come to love. Well, it was so neat because that song became my first big hit. It really got things going for me career-wise, and it was all because we wrote about something real.

I love Kelley's story about the first time he took McCain fishing. He and Karen were still just dating at the time, and they took a weekend trip to visit Karen's parents, Faye and Dub, in Sand Mountain, Alabama. When they got there, Kelley noticed this pond on their property. It was way back out of the way and kind of overgrown. Kelley asked Dub if there were fish in there. Dub answered him in his deep Southern drawl, "Oh, yeah! Tharintharuptoyerarm!"

Kelley knew this was good. So Kelley gathered up some rods and took McCain, who was only three years old at the time, down to the pond. They found a place to stand on the shore, and Kelley gave McCain a small rod baited with a plastic worm. He told him to go ahead and drop in his line.

Kelley wasn't sure if McCain, who stood about as tall as Kelley's waist, would be able to work the artificial worm. They didn't have any live bait, but McCain didn't seem to mind. He wasn't paying much attention anyway. Kelley just figured he'd give him something to do.

McCain seemed content, so Kelley wasn't worried about him. He started concentrating on his own tactics. He tried deep-dive crank bait, then a plastic worm, then a lizard. Kelley tried all these different things. After about fifteen minutes or so, McCain quietly announced, "I got one."

Kelley didn't think he really had a fish because the pole wasn't bent. Anyway, he told him, "OK, Buddy. Reel it in."

So McCain reels up slowly while Kelley is still turned away, thinking about hooking a fish. Then he looks over and sees McCain pulling in a three-and-a-half pound bass! This was huge for a three-year-old kid. It would have been huge for anybody.

Kelley said McCain didn't even have the fish fully hooked. The bass had its mouth enclosed around the worm and kept holding on as McCain gently pulled him up out of the water. There was no fight to it at all!

Kelley looked over at McCain and said, "How did you do that?" The fish was just lying there docile as could be. Kelley lipped it and picked it up. The fish kind of shook when he did that.

Well, McCain sees his mom and grandma up on the driveway and starts yelling, "Mama! Mama! Look what I caught!"

Here's Kelley, who had bragged to Karen, his new girlfriend, that he had been fishing all his life. He's empty-handed while McCain whips up this three-and-a-half pound bass like it's nothing! Well, they released the fish, which happened to be the only one they got that day.

When they got back to the house, everyone kept asking Kelley, "What'd y'all catch?"

Kelley told them they didn't have a very good day. Then little McCain pipes up, "Well, we just caught that one."

"I'm Gonna Miss Her"

Fishing is Brad Paisley's passion. (It edges out music, which is his number-one pursuit, only because that is his job). Speaking of passions . . . what about love? Paisley gave a clue about love's ranking while on tour in the summer of 2001, when he added his new song, "I'm Gonna Miss Her," to his show.

He sang: "I love her . . . but I love to fish . . ." After just these few words, the audience burst into laughter and applause. They knew where this song was going. (Later, the fans sent this song to number one.) The fishermen in the audience and their fishing widows recognized the scenario instantly. Surely this self-described romantic did not write this song from personal experience.

This is definitely a true story. I was in a relationship way back when. One day, I told my girlfriend that we would go out to dinner. We made the plans that morning, so there was plenty of time for fishing during the day. I was out on the boat with a guy who was dating my girlfriend's friend. It was a really good day on the lake, and we were actually catching a lot of fish. I took him with me to win points. Like I was doing something for her. Also, on the off chance we would be late, I'd have him with me. He was like insurance. My girl was even hanging out with that guy's girlfriend, her friend, that day. So, what could go wrong?

Well, we stayed out a lot longer than we should have, but we just couldn't go in. I didn't get to her house until dark, and I still had the boat hooked up. I got there and hadn't showered, hadn't gotten ready, and here we are. I show up, and she's ready to go to sleep. I wasn't even let in. She just came to the door and said, "Look. This isn't working."

Brad onstage in Branson, Missouri

Really, I think men and women can relate to this situation whether the concern is a guy golfing too much or watching football on TV. It's not just about fishing. But I meant the song to be fun and playful. Definitely tongue in cheek. When we perform it, women are probably the biggest fans of this song. I'm trying to say that guys are just a bunch of idiots, and we know it.

It's funny because I never had this song pegged as the one that would become my biggest hit. I wrote it with Frank Rogers when we were still students at Belmont University. I had a writer's night coming up. It was a small show where you get to showcase your songs. I remember it was a Wednesday night, and the show was coming up on Saturday. Frank and I were going over my set list. He said, "You've got some great songs here, but they're all ballads. Most of them are kind of sad too. We've got to have something on here that's not going to put them to sleep. Something with a smile on it!"

So, I pulled out the beginnings of a song with this same kind of idea that I'd started in high school. Then we wrote "I'm Gonna Miss Her." All for one show just to make people laugh.

I was surprised at how well it went over. I mean, at first we were afraid we might offend some people. And I know some people may not like it. A Southwest Airlines ticket agent noticed my dad's last name when he was making a flight reservation and said, "By the way, I hate that song." (She got him a good price anyway.)

But that night, for the most part, guys and girls got it right away. Right from the first line. Everybody laughed. Oh, they liked the depressing songs I was so proud of, too. But this one was the crowd-pleaser.

Not too long after that, we had a demo session where we recorded eight songs. It was the end of the day. Everybody was tired. But we decided since we had everybody there to go ahead and cut the fishing song real quick, just to have it on tape.

Well, we ended up turning in the demo of the song with all the other songs we recorded. The next thing we know, the song was on hold for George Strait, Garth Brooks, and Alan Jackson! We couldn't believe it.

Well, none of them cut the song. Alan had it on hold, meaning he intended to record it, for eight or nine months. He finally went in the studio to do it. He had planned on recording eleven songs, but ended up only cutting ten. "I'm Gonna Miss Her" is the one he didn't do.

Not long after that, I got my record deal at Arista. In fact, the deal came from the demo that included the fishing song. I was just trying to sell a song, but the label said, "Well, I guess that guy doesn't sing so bad."

Anyway, I was glad I still had the song. I knew I'd end up doing it on my second record. It wasn't really right for the first one. I didn't want people to hear it and think of me as a novelty act.

So, after my first album came out, Alan Jackson called again and said, "Hey, what about that fishing song?" He wanted it back. I said, "Heck, no!"

I felt a sense of fate with this song. I wanted to sing it because I love to fish. The most rewarding thing to me is to listen to the crowd sing the chorus back to me like an anthem. I love it. I guess every once in a while it's good to sing a song that doesn't make you want to kill yourself.

Even before this song was on the radio, when I played it in concert the fans reacted to it like it was a hit. That's why I was so adamant about it being a single. When you see a song go over like that in front of an audience, you've just got to think it's going to translate to radio. You don't get a chance at that kind of song very often, and I owe it all to fishing.

So, now that I sing this song all the time, everybody wants to know if my fiancé, Kim, and I go fishing. We definitely do. She loves it. She actually likes going out there, though not all day like I do. It's more of a boat ride for her.

I think it's great she likes to go. But the thing is, she's yet to catch a fish! I told her, "Boy, you're *really* going to love this if you can ever catch one." I don't know if she doesn't care or if it's because she isn't really doing it right. I keep telling her things like let the lure sink a little more, or set the hook. People who are new at fishing don't like to set their hooks because they think they will pull the lure out of the water. And she's not looking forward to taking the hook out of the fish's mouth. But I told her, don't worry about that. That's a good problem to have. I would be inclined to help with that. But she says she really likes casting. I say, "Well, that's good, but we can do that in the backyard!"

Actually, I think it's a good thing when your girlfriend or your wife doesn't necessarily love fishing as much as you do. Otherwise, you'll end up fighting when you're taking off with the guys. You know, "Why aren't you taking me? Why can't I go?"

That's a whole other argument. One you don't want to have.

It's Not Called Catching . . . It's Called Fishing

Even though Brad Paisley made his mark with fishermen with a song about choosing fishing over a girl, we know his tongue was in his cheek. First of all, we know by now he chose the girl. And Brad knows plenty of women love to fish. It just might surprise you who some of these women happen to be.

Say the name "Mary Ann," and people immediately think of the cute brunette with the pigtails who made all those great coconut creme pies on the TV show *Gilligan's Island*. Everybody knows Mary Ann. But most people probably don't know that the actress who played her, Dawn Wells, is also an accomplished fly fisherman. She says her favorite T-shirt sports the message: "I Fish, Therefore I Am." That says a lot about a woman!

She also lived in Nashville for fourteen years and fished for bass in the same lakes that I do! But she grew up out west in Nevada and used to head to Idaho and Wyoming to fly fish for rainbow trout with her father. Later, long after *Gilligan's Island* went off the air, she even co-produced and hosted her own fishing show, *Dawn Wells' Reel Adventures*, which aired in Canada a few years ago. Her cohost was Kathy Ruddick, who was the first female captain of the Canadian Fly Fishing Team. They put together thirteen episodes and traveled all over the world fishing in Canada, Mexico, Scotland, and Iceland.

Dawn says she's not a great angler, which is hard to believe if you saw the show where she caught a huge salmon on a fly rod! Dawn had a really

Dawn Wells in Driggs, Idaho

close relationship with her father. He used to tell her she could do anything she set her mind to. When she said, "Daddy, I don't know how to tie this!" He would answer, "Ah! You can do that!"

She took his lesson to heart. She knows she can do it. But when she says she's not a great angler, I think she means she has never been one to catch a lot of fish. Especially when she was little.

She says she remembers being out on the river with her dad, sitting on the front of the boat. As soon as she slapped the water, the fish would scatter. Her dad, on the other hand, would get one every time he put the rod in! But he would always make her feel better by saying, "It's not called 'catching'. It's called 'fishing'." A lot of anglers—both men and women—understand that. There's a lot more to fishing than just volume.

For Dawn, fishing is about communication with nature and being out in the solitude and the quiet. She says fishing restores something in her soul. I know what she means. It's a little surprising, but after her dad passed away in 1967, Dawn didn't spend much time in Idaho. Then in 1994 she traveled back to Driggs, Idaho, which is at the foot of the Teton Mountains, and realized how much she missed it. All her memories came flooding back. The town was still about the same size. It was still as tranquil as she remembered.

So, she got herself a lodge and opened her Film Actors Boot Camp right there in the Teton Valley. When she's not too busy teaching actors how to behave on and off stage, she heads out to one of her favorite streams, often with her nephew who makes his own rods and ties his own flies. These days they release all the fish they catch. But every time Dawn hits the river, she remembers the days years ago when she would stop by the side of the streams with her dad to cook the trout they caught. It always makes her feel at peace to think of those times, except maybe the one time she hooked her stepmother on the lip with a fly. (Dawn says she was a good sport about it, especially since it didn't leave a scar!)

Dawn also has incredible memories of filming her show. She learned that in Iceland people rent part of the river when they fish. Including the cost of the guide, it can run anglers $700 a day. They really value their pristine environment there, so that's one way of taking care of it. In some places, you can only take four fish a day!

Besides keeping places from getting over fished, the other result is that fishing is considered an upscale activity. Dawn said the same was true in Scotland. A dignitary named Lady Catherine joined her for filming and came dressed in little knickers and a cashmere vest— evidently she couldn't believe that Americans wore T-shirts and jeans to go fishing!

Anyway, Dawn had her mom, who is now in her nineties, with her in Iceland. They were way north of Reykjavik. When they got out on the river, Dawn landed a twenty-pound salmon which, since they were filming a show, they would hold up and show to the cameras. Well, every time they did that, Dawn got nervous. Being of the catch-and-release school, she knew there were only so many minutes the fish could survive out of the water.

So Dawn pulled in this twenty-pounder, and while Kathy was showing her how to aerate the fish and get it moving back in the water, she said she looked down at it and realized she had his life in her hands.

Tears started coming down her face! She said it surprised her after all these years of fishing to feel that way, but she got really emotional. Maybe she was thinking about her mom? The Icelanders couldn't understand why they were putting the fish back. They pay a lot of money to fish! They eat them! They certainly didn't understand why Dawn was so emotional.

Dawn loves to cook fish, too. Especially the just-out-of-river stuff. It may sound like a contradiction, but I get it. I think she's just another fisherman who loves and respects the environment and the living creatures in it.

Makes sense to me.

Fishing: The Movie

Ever since MTV, VH1, and CMT hit the tube, country singers have gotten the chance to polish their acting chops. When they manage to write a hit song or a tune their record company perceives has the potential to be a hit song, they get to make a mini-movie—a video. Sometimes the star gets involved in producing, casting, and directing. If they have vision. And the right inspiration.

Once we knew "I'm Gonna Miss Her" (The Fishin' Song) was going to be a single, I got busy thinking about the video we would make. It's funny, I think I saw the whole thing playing in my head way before we even started. I can't believe it came together like we wanted it to.

The first obstacle was my record company president, Joe Galante. I went to him with the idea of illustrating my song by doing a fake *Jerry Springer* show and patching in to an ESPN fishing tournament, using all my friends as actors. He sat down and basically told me all the reasons this was a really bad idea. But I just kept calling people, like Dan Patrick from ESPN, who it turns out was a fan of my music. He had my album.

So, over Christmas, I drove up to Connecticut to see him. He's a big fly fisherman. But more than that, he's just into having a good time. He's a really neat guy. He got the concept. And he did a great job. He filmed his whole part at the ESPN Studios in Connecticut.

Then, I called Jerry Springer. He's a huge country music fan. He's even working on his own record! I hadn't heard him sing, but I offered to do something on his record. Either play guitar or write a song. He said not to worry about that. He just wanted to do the video. So, he was excited.

When Jerry first heard "I'm Gonna Miss Her," he says he got it right away. He got the joke—he just didn't relate. He kept teasing me, "So, if the choice is a woman or a fish, you're choosing a fish? Call me crazy. I've never been excited by a fish."

Jerry admitted that maybe he didn't have a full appreciation of fishing. In fact, he confessed the only time he had ever caught a fish was when the guy at the supermarket tossed one to him right before he paid for it at the checkout counter. But the important thing is that he understood the man-woman conflict. To some degree, that's what every one of his shows is really about, once you get down deep.

Brad Paisley being interviewed by Jerry Springer while filming the "I'm Gonna Miss Her" video

So, for Jerry's part of the video, the pseudo-*Springer* show, "Men Who Choose Fishing Over Love," we recreated his whole vibe on a soundstage in Nashville. He flew down, and we had a great time. We basically did a whole Jerry Springer show by the time we were done.

The "actors" were all my friends. The four fishermen featured on the show were Kelley Lovelace, Frank Rogers, Tim Owens, and Little Jimmy Dickens. The four wives were their real-life wives: Karen Lovelace, Jessica Rogers, Paula Owens, and Mona Dickens. Those are all my best friends up there with their real wives.

When we started taping, all the wives just started complaining and yelling at their husbands. There were definitely some frustrations taken out in this scene. We didn't have any balsa wood chairs, so we skipped that part. But it sure felt real.

Jerry agreed. He said it was funny how when the cameras started rolling, no one had to be coached on how to behave. He pulled me aside and laughed, "Ya know, Brad. It dawned on me that every one of these people has a story that would have made our show. During the breaks, they keep whispering to me, 'Boy have I got a story for you!'"

Possibly the best part (I'm biased) of the video was down in Alabama when we taped the fishing tournament. Hank Parker, the TV show host, and Forrest Wood, the founder of Ranger Boats, made cameos. Hank was really into this. Forrest got into it too. He's the one I'm buying the fish from in the scene where Dan says, "He's cheating!"

The best part was we did a whole day of fishing. I brought Kelley, Frank, and Tim as my fishing buddies. Not much acting involved there! We weren't about to be on a lake like that and not throw in some lines. Luckily, we needed the footage for the video. We caught a bunch of fish that day too. I think we got seventy-something fish among us. I guess when you have the right inspiration . . .

The key to the video, of course, is the girl. The one I sort of leave behind when she asks me to choose between her and fishing. The girl who played my wife in the video is my fiancé, Kimberly Williams. She was the only real actor on the set! She starred in *The Father of the Bride* movies and also stars on the ABC sitcom *According to Jim*, with Jim Belushi.

She is a great actress. As soon as she did her thing, my jaw hit the floor. Here's Kelley, Karen, Frank and his wife, and me, all trying to act. Then it was Kimberly's turn. I just said, "Whoa! I guess that'll do."

People still come up to me and tell me their favorite part of the video is when Kimberly hits me on the head. We had to do that take like nine

Brad Paisley and Kimberly Williams on the "I'm Gonna Miss Her" video shoot

times because I kept laughing. But it hurt! It wasn't fake. She was actually hitting me in the back of the head pretty hard.

I guess we could have tried that fake, actor-slap thing they do. But for that to work, both the people need to be actors and know what they're doing. So that wouldn't work. I had to get hit. I think she was enjoying it a little too much.

Doing this video was one of the coolest experiences. I got to work with all my friends. That was the best part. But I think the video really helped the song reach number one. The director, Peter Zavadil, really hit this one out of the park. (He calls me a "massive fishing fanatic.") The video won some awards too. We got Best Concept Video at the CMT Flameworthy Awards. That was really neat because the fans vote for that. We also got the 2002 CMA Video of the Year award.

I'm glad I'll be able to watch it for years and years. It makes me laugh every time. I mean, did you see Little Jimmy during the fight scene?

Snakes & Snails

There's something about little boys and snakes. As the poem goes, it's part of what they are made of.

When I was growing up, my mom used to say, "Brad gets so attached to things." I guess that's true. We went to the beach one summer, and I was really fascinated by those little crabs that burrow into the sand. I thought they were the neatest things. I begged my parents to let me bring some home. They said no at first, telling me they wouldn't live. Well, they ended up letting me bring a couple home, and sure enough, when we opened the trunk they were goners.

Mom also said I liked anything as long as it was "alive and slimy." I don't think she liked it much, but I used to bring home snakes. I was really into snakes as a kid. My friends and I would go out and collect them along the river near our house. Nothing poisonous, like copperheads or rattlers. They were water snakes. Little snakes. Well, most of them were.

One time, I guess I was in the third grade, I brought home a three-and-a-half-foot black snake, and it got loose. It turned into a neighborhood crisis! Everybody came out to try to help catch this huge thing. It was nighttime, and we probably had forty-five people in our back yard with the lights on. Someone saw it crawl under a bush, then it was by the garage. We had it surrounded, but it got past all of us.

Then, we saw it slither up this really huge tree. My friends and I just sat around the base of the tree for like four hours waiting for it to come down. But it didn't. It could've stayed up there for weeks.

Brad Paisley with his first fish

Actually, I kind of made a habit of losing snakes. Since I liked to bring them home so much, I built an all-glass cage for them that my dad made me keep in the garage. He wouldn't let me keep it in the house, which made me mad at the time, but looking back I guess I can understand.

Well, I used to bring them home and put them in the cage. One day, my dad is out in the garage. He didn't really like snakes, but he wasn't deathly afraid of them either. But he was definitely startled when he saw the door of my snake cage wide open and no snakes inside.

He said, "Hey, Brad. Where are your snakes?" My eyes went wide, and I took off like a bat. I had forgotten to put the door down, and all my snakes were gone. To this day, my mom and dad still stop and look around every time they go into the garage.

After a while, I kind of graduated from snake collecting and went on to get serious about fishing. As soon as my buddies and I perfected our bait, we were ready to head out across the railroad tracks, across the grass runway of the tiny airport in our town, and make our way down to the river in search of fish. Our secret bait, something we were sure the catfish and the carp would love, was a mix of whatever we could find at home in our moms' kitchens. We called our creations *dough balls*.

They were made up of flour, salt, corn, water, and sometimes cheese, or whatever else inspired us. I'm telling you, the fish, especially the carp, loved them. They ate 'em up. Don't tell Hank Parker.

Skipping a Generation

Brad grew up in Glen Dale, West Virginia, a Mayberryesque (pop. 1800) Ohio River town. His parents, Doug and Sandy Paisley, were always supportive. But it was his grandfather, Warren Jarvis, who had the most direct influence on young Brad. His grandfather gave him his first guitar, a Sears Danelectro Silvertone with an amp in the case. They would play music together. Then Brad would beg him to go fishing.

While I was growing up, I spent every afternoon after school with my grandfather. He was always teaching. No matter what I would do, he was always trying his best to make sure that I knew what he wanted me to know. It never ended. He could talk forever. I often thought he missed his calling—he should have been a teacher rather than an engineer.

He'd give me advice. Miscellaneous odds and ends like, "Don't ever go to your grave owing anybody anything." He would pull quotes out of nowhere. He was the kind of guy who would see me sitting eating breakfast and would say, "Brad, you know, here's the trick: Don't go to your grave owing anybody anything." It was always very interesting that he would come up with these things over bacon and eggs. It continued when I fished with him. Things like the Golden Rule or sayings from the Bible. He was always misquoting the Bible. Although he was close most of the time, he was usually only 90 percent correct. It was interesting to grow up with him.

To this day, I can't sleep if I've borrowed money and haven't paid it back because I hear him saying, "Don't go to your grave owing anybody anything." I remember, when I was a little kid, I would go to the local drug store to buy a comic book. One time, I was ten cents short. Since I was in that store every day, the lady behind the counter said, "Just take it home. You wanted this book and came all the way up here to get it. You can pay me next time you're in here." Great. I went home and was eating dinner when my mom noticed that she hadn't given me enough for it. I didn't tell her either. I was going to pay the lady back somehow. She said, "What are you doing? This cost more than you had." I said, "Well, she let me have it and said that I could pay her later." So she picked me up from the dinner table, put me in a car, drove me to the drug store, and made me pay the lady.

She actually got mad at me! It's funny, because I look back and realize it was one of those real Andy and Opie moments where you don't really think you're doing anything wrong. I really wasn't planning on keeping it. But I was a little kid. It was only ten cents. But it was the principle of the thing. I learned a big lesson that day.

My grandfather used to talk about catching crappy and drum down on the river in Huntington when he was young. He lived a very Huck Finn/Tom Sawyer life as a kid. He was a rebel and would run from things. He would skip school to go fishing a lot. I don't think he even got through the ninth grade. Later, he was sent to World War II, and while stationed in the Army in the Philippines, he learned Morse code and dispatching. He worked in the air fields, and that experience gave him his trade. When he got back to the United States, he was hired by the railroad and worked for them until he retired. It was something that really didn't need school. But he was very wise, much more than most people who go to college.

On the other hand, I never skipped school to go fishing! Unless I had permission. I skipped one afternoon for a couple of hours, but I never took off and lied about it. My mom was a teacher at the local grade school, and my uncle taught at the high school. It would have been a matter of minutes before someone noticed me missing. My uncle or somebody probably would have talked to my parents and said, "Oh, is Brad sick?" It wouldn't have worked.

The most memorable fishing trip of my life was the last time I went with my grandfather before he died. He had cancer. We walked down to the Ohio River and threw in a line. He caught the biggest fish I had ever seen him catch. I'd say it was about a ten-pound carp—it was huge. It was the last time we fished together. It was a great memory.

We carried the fish home and stuck it in the rain barrel that was part of the downspout off my grandparents' porch. We plugged up the hole so it would stay full of water. And the fish lived!

That night, I think my grandfather was feeling bad the fish wasn't in the lake. I mean, it was so big, it really couldn't swim around in the barrel. It just kind of rolled around sideways. So, he went outside in the dark, got the fish out of the rain barrel, took it back down to the river and threw it back in. I had already gone to bed. I didn't even know he'd done it. It was perfect.

A lot of guys, like me, tell stories about their grandfathers teaching them to fish. Well, for my friend Tracy Byrd, it was his grandmother, Nana, who taught him to fish—and hunt too. They had an incredible relationship.

Tracy spent every holiday and weekend with her from the time he was four years old till he left for college. She did all the things grandmas did: she was an incredible cook, and she could sew and knit. But to some degree, she was more like a grandfather than she was a grandmother.

Tracy's grandfather died when he was two, so he never really knew him. But even when he was alive, it was Nana who was the avid out-doorswoman. She loved it! When she was young, her family was so poor they farmed, hunted, and fished just to survive. She never tasted a piece of beef until she was in her teens, because they lived on deer, squirrel, rabbits, and catfish. The byproduct of that was that not only was she great at going out and finding things—harvesting game and catching fish—but she could cook it better than anybody.

So when he was growing up in Texas, Tracy got to go hunting with Nana for deer, duck, and squirrel. She ran trout lines. She even trapped! Then she would cure and sell the hides. That was part of the way she made her living. She had this big farm and grew vegetables. And she had a sawmill where she contracted out work.

Her other side-job was a lawn care business. In the summertime, Tracy went with her. It was hard work, but they had a ball together.

In the summer before Tracy went into the fifth grade, it was their last day of working together. They were trying to finish everything so they could take off for two weeks. Just the two of them were going to Toledo Bend. They planned to pitch a tent and take Nana's aluminum bass boat

Tracy Byrd with Kevin Van Dam

with the ten horsepower motor and bass fish all day long. They planned to set out trout lines too. Tracy couldn't have been more excited about this trip.

It was 6:30 in the morning of the day they were supposed to leave. They arrived at the Bonus Burger, to cut the grass. Nana says, "Tracy, you get the push mower. I'm gonna mow all the big stuff out back. You mow all those ditches in the front." Tracy said OK. He was used to doing the ditches.

Tracy got busy mowing the first ditch. He'd push the mower down and pull it back out, up and down. The thing was, there was dew on the grass, and his right foot slipped and went underneath the mower. It cut the front off his old Nike tennis shoes with the aqua blue stripe and caught his big toe. It just cut it. It was hanging there like a piece of meat.

Through all the pain and everything, all Tracy could think of was, "Dang! I'm not going to get to go on the fishing trip!"

He killed the lawnmower and staggered over to his grandmother. She was going in circles, not paying any attention. He hollered at her. His toe was bleeding. Finally, he got her attention. She saw what happened and freaked out. She jumped in the truck and took off without him! She sort of lost her mind for a minute. Then she realized what she was doing, backed up and said, "Get in the dang truck!"

They went to the hospital, and the doctors sewed up Tracy's toe. While they were wrapping his entire foot and ankle, Tracy said, "Doc, we're going on a fishing trip." The doctor told him, "Boy, you don't need to be going on no fishing trip." He said his foot needed to be elevated for at least five days. And he wasn't supposed to walk on it. In fact, he needed a crutch.

Tracy begged him. Then Nana jumped in. "Is there anyway he can go fishing?"

The doctor asked if there was a seat in the boat and a place to elevate his foot, like on an ice chest or something. Nana said there was.

So, they left the next morning. They spent two weeks at the lake with Tracy's foot all wrapped up and propped on the ice chest. He would sit there and cast just like that! Using his old Rappalla, broken-minnow floater—his secret lure the summer before fifth grade. When they got home, his toe was pretty much healed.

Call it bass therapy. He took the cure.

Tracy says when he thinks of his grandmother now (she passed away in the spring of 2001), he thinks of her patience. She was a great teacher. Even though she had to hunt and fish for survival when she was growing up, she fell in love with the outdoors anyway. She loved trying to outsmart the game and staying on fish.

Tracy says she was patient with him because she got to a point where it brought her more joy to introduce people to the sport than it did doing it herself. She had shifted to where teaching was her goal. She wanted him to fall in love with it and leave some of her know-how with him. That's exactly how my grandfather was with me.

Tracy has three little kids. He says he hasn't quite reached that selfless point. He still can't get enough of fishing and still dreams about catching the big one. But he's starting to see that part of him coming out when he takes his daughter and two young sons to his beach house on the Gulf of Mexico. They take his boat out, and he's sure to put the big T-top on it to give his kids some shade. They anchor and catch speckled trout and redfish. Sometimes, he doesn't even fish. He just watches and helps them.

Saturday Mornings with Jimmy

Jimmy Houston is as well known for his lightened-by-the-sun blonde hair and his unmistakable laugh as he is for his fishing prowess. Anglers have been waking up to his show, Jimmy Houston Outdoors, *for twenty-five years. He's had an unbeatable career as a tournament fisherman and has been given countless honors, including his induction into the National Fresh-Water Fishing Hall of Fame. And he is rumored to be a tremendous human being.*

Like all guys who love to fish, I grew up watching Jimmy Houston's show. I still watch it. I'm really excited because we just got TiVo, the new digital satellite service, on our tour bus. That means we can automatically tape his show, even with the TV off. Then in the middle of the night, when me and the guys in the band are wide awake and there's nothing but infomercials, we can watch Jimmy! It's going to be great.

Other people idolize NASCAR drivers, actors, or whatever, but I've always been a really big fan of these guys on TV, like Jimmy, who catch fish day in and day out. I'm a bit of a groupie to these fishing guys. I want their job! I want to endorse fishing products and give people tips.

Jimmy says fishing for a living is a lot more difficult than people think. You have to put a lot into it to get anything out of it.

Jimmy Houston on the river

When he hears me say I want his job he says, "It's not too bad standing up there singing for a living either!" True. I'm not complaining. But personally, I think fishing would be a fun way to make a living. To *have to* fish!

These guys are just legendary. There are a select few that have become fishing icons—Jimmy Houston is one of them. He's just so recognizable with that blonde mop on top of his head. And the laugh! Jimmy is as good a guy as you'd hope he'd be. He has a very strong Christian faith, and one of his books, *Hooked for Life*, compares Bible lessons to fishing. I keep that book at my house for people who visit!

The first time I met Jimmy was at a taping for a TNN show, *The Wonders of Wildlife*. He and his wife, Chris, were there. I went up and introduced myself to Chris and asked her to introduce me to Jimmy. I was so excited to meet him. Not that he was intimidating. I mean, fishing-show guys don't have bodyguards or road managers around to make it difficult. But I was definitely in awe of him. So I went through her. They both put me at ease right away.

He and Chris are a great team and an inspiration in a lot of ways, not just as fishing people, but as a couple. They're a great example to people, especially to someone like me who sings about the difficulties of relationships. They're the opposite of all that. They've been married for forty years, and they have what everybody wants. I love watching them together.

Chris is a champion angler herself. She was the top woman on the pro circuit for years! She fished every Bass'n'Gal Tournament there was. I think if she were asked to choose between fishing and her husband, she'd probably leave him! Seriously, they are delightful.

Jimmy says fishing is like golf, it has caused a lot of problems with marriages. But then there are guys like him who end up getting their girlfriends or wives involved in fishing, and not only do the girls like it, but they become a guy's best fishing partner.

Jimmy and Chris have fished together forever—right from the beginning. He tells great stories about them going on fishing dates. When they first hooked up (pun intended), Jimmy was a senior in high school and Chris was a freshman.

Chris had a really strict curfew. Jimmy had to have her home by ten unless they were, uh . . . fishing. Jimmy worked his way through college selling catfish. They used to catfish a lot at night. Of course, that was way before professional fishing or pro bass tournaments came along, and there were no such things as fishing shows yet. One night, Jimmy and Chris stayed up all night and caught 153 catfish! Obviously, that was way over the limit—I think you're allowed fifteen in Oklahoma, where they lived. Anyway, they caught so many that they ran out of bait. Jimmy's mom and dad owned a resort on Lake Tinkiller where they were fishing, so Jimmy went in and got the keys to the store, opened it up, and got some more bait. (They were using stink bait or what Jimmy calls Catfish Charlie). Then they went back out and stayed out all night.

Jimmy says at first he was so naïve, he didn't realize he could keep her out that late without going fishing. If they went to the drive-in or something, he'd have to have her home by ten o'clock. But after about a year, he finally caught on. He said, "Hey! I can go out, fish until dark or so, and catch a mess of fish. Then I'll pick her up and keep her on a date as long as I want! As long as I brought home a bunch of fish to her mama, it'd be OK!"

They dated for two and a half years, then they got married. Then they really started bringing home the fish.

I haven't gotten a chance to fish with Jimmy yet for one of his shows, but I swear it's going to happen soon! He has taken out so many anglers over the years, I know they all blend together for him. Even the famous ones. But incredibly, several stories of fellow singer-fishermen are fresh in his mind.

He told me that Bobby Bare is the most laid-back fisherman he's ever seen. A lot of people would say fishing is mellow by definition, but I don't really think so. Anyone who has ever seen a tournament fisherman knows they can be pretty hard charging. Many of them don't even carry a front seat in the boat, and they fish from daylight to dark. Intense.

Jimmy Houston on the lake

But Jimmy tells me Bobby Bare is the complete opposite—the epitome of relaxation fishing. He sort of melts into the back seat of a Ranger boat and almost casts from a lying-down position. He's a pretty good fisherman, according to Jimmy, but he's really, really mellow.

"He's a pretty laid-back guy in regular life," Jimmy says. "But when he goes fishing, he squeezes all the relaxation out of it he can. He's one of those guys who goes fishing and hopes he doesn't get a bite because it will distract from the relaxation in the great outdoors."

With an attitude like that, who needs yoga?

Jimmy has also spent a lot of time with Jeff Cook, the lead guitarist for the band Alabama. He says it cracks him up when Jeff calls the office and one of the girls in the office says, "Some guy called from Alabama."

One summer, Jimmy went down to Fort Payne to emcee Alabama's June Jam, and afterward, he and Jeff went fishing. They fished all day until about four in the afternoon. Jeff left and went up to his house. Jimmy was loading the boat, when all of the sudden it started raining. He got soaking wet. He walked to Jeff's house all wet and muddy, with his hair all matted, and peeked his head inside to ask where he should park the boat.

This "grandma looking lady," as he put it, starts jumping up and down and carrying on, "Oh, Jimmy! I can't believe it! It's you! Carl and I never miss your show."

Well, Jimmy was gracious as he could be, all drippy as he was. He just thought this woman was Jeff's aunt or something and "Carl" was his uncle. Then Jeff's wife introduced them. Turns out, Carl was none other than Carl Perkins. Jimmy couldn't believe it! This giant of rock-and-roll was a fan of his show!

"You never know who's watching those shows on Saturday mornings," Jimmy laughs.

A Man and His Boat

It has been said, the boat doesn't make the man. But it doesn't hurt. It's not about the horsepower. Or the size. Or the shine. What's important is that it's equipped for fishing. And that you can call it your own.

Getting my first boat was a big event. It's a really big deal to a guy. When I was growing up in West Virginia, we had a boat. A cheap one. It was a piece of junk, really. It had like a seventy-horsepower motor. I learned to ski off it, and we did that all the time. But it was a flat-paint, mustard-yellow Tri-hull. Really bad! It didn't ride very well, but I guess it did the trick.

After a year or two in Nashville, I had my first success as a song-writer. David Kersh recorded my song called "Another You" and made it a big hit. The first check I got for that was pretty big compared to anything I'd ever seen before. It was five figures big! I remember thinking, *Boy, I know what I'm doing with this. It's time for a boat.*

I looked in the trade magazines and the classifieds. Mainly, I looked for a good deal. I was interested in a Ranger. The nice thing about Rangers, which can also be a Catch-22, is that they tend to hold their value more than other boats.

Brad Paisley fishing in Branson, Missouri

So an older Ranger will cost about the same as another brand's newer model. But that didn't bother me. It would be new to me. And it would be a Ranger. So I bought an '88 Ranger, which was seven years old at the time. That was the best boat I could get for my money. I still have it, actually. Well, I gave it to Tim Owens to keep when Ranger— my tour sponsor now—gave me a new one.

I like knowing that that boat is still around. It's a really important boat to me because I learned a lot of things on it! When I was just a songwriter,

I would spend so many days out on that boat. Before I had a record deal, I think I fished a hundred days a year. And it was just great! I had it bad!

I lived in a condo at the time, and there wasn't room for me to keep the boat there. So I kept it in storage about eight miles away. In order to charge the two batteries, I had to unload them out of the boat every time I came off the lake. It was unbelievable!

In order to take the boat out, I had to go get the batteries off my back porch, drive down to where my boat was stored, take it out, hook it up, and put the batteries back in. Keep in mind these are fifty-pound batteries. Then I would drive over to the lake.

So every time I had the urge to fish, which was often, I had to take the boat out of storage, stop by my condo, pick up the batteries, and then go fishing. When I returned, I had to stop by my condo, take the batteries out of it again, carry them onto the back porch of my condo, then take the boat back and put it in storage, then cover the boat because it was outdoor storage. So I would literally put a cover on it, its actual cover, then I would put two tarps on it and wrap them up. Sometimes I'd do that a couple days in a row!

It was really hard to do. Then as soon as I could afford it, I bought a house, the same one I live in now. Before I even considered buying it, I measured the garage to make sure my boat would fit in there. And it barely fit!

My '88 Ranger is an eighteen-foot boat. It needed exactly twenty-three feet of space. My garage is twenty-three feet and six inches. So with the door down, you have to step over the tongue of the trailer. But it fits.

It's funny, when I was getting ready to close on the house, I had already measured the garage and I knew the boat fit. But I told the guy, I've measured it and I know it fits, but it's close enough that there is a slight chance that I'll pull it in there and it won't work. If it doesn't fit, I don't want to be obligated. He said OK. I even put it in the contract.

So I bought the house. The first thing I did was go and get my boat! I stuck it in the garage right away. It fit! The best part was the feeling of just being able to keep the batteries in the boat and plug in a charger.

Brad on Percy Priest Lake, Nashville, Tennessee

So now it's much easier to take out the boat but much harder to find the time. I guess I just feel better knowing it's right there!

Last summer, Ranger boats sponsored my tour. It was great. We incorporated an entire eighteen-foot boat into the set. It was put right on the stage. The keyboard guy actually sat right in the boat. And the drummer sat on the dock. I didn't spend much time in the boat on stage. But like I said, I just like knowing my boat is nearby.

In Your Dreams

On February 17, 2001, Brad Paisley stood on the wooden stage of the historic Ryman Auditorium in downtown Nashville, Tennessee. He looked up at the four-story high stained-glass windows and got chills thinking of the legendary country singers who had played on this stage before him. Hank Williams, Johnny Cash, Willie Nelson, Patsy Cline. That night his lifelong dream was fulfilled when he was inducted into the Grand Ole Opry.

For Brad, this was an enormous personal accomplishment. Most artists play the Opry for years before being asked to become a member. Brad did it in just over one year. Remarkably, he was just twenty-eight years old.

It isn't all dreaming, picking, and grinning on that Opry stage, though. Seems some of the performers on the nation's longest-running radio program have more than history and music on their minds. They're thinking about the one that got away.

One of the best days I've ever had was when Kelley Lovelace, my best friend and songwriting partner, and I went fishing with Grand Ole Opry star Little Jimmy Dickens. We took him up to a pond by Kelley's in-laws' place at Sand Mountain, Alabama.

We were so excited to be going with him. In a way, he's just like every other guy who likes to fish. He fishes all the time. But this guy is an Opry legend. We couldn't get that out of our minds.

Before we thought about driving to Alabama, we had to gear up for our trip. That's part of the fun of fishing. It's not just a trip, it's an event. So you have to be well supplied. In Nashville, I go to Bass Pro Shops a lot. I can get lost in there. You could lock me in, and I'd be fine for a couple of hours. If they locked the doors, I wouldn't know.

It's a blast getting your tackle together before you go. I tend to over-purchase. I might spend two hundred dollars on stuff and use thirty-dollars worth of it. Not to mention the boat. It's not exactly an economical way to "buy" your fish. It would average out to about thirty dollars a pound! You're never gonna break even. But that's not the point.

We knew Little Jimmy loved to fish. First of all, he talked about it all the time. And, Jimmy Houston told me that he and Little Jimmy fished together once up at Truman Lake in Missouri. Big Jimmy said he knew Little Jimmy loved to fish when he was willing to drive all the way up to Truman early the next morning after a late-night show!

Little Jimmy says that when he's on stage, his mind is on the job. (He's not like me, always working out schemes to catch bigger fish.) But the minute he comes off stage, he's ready to go fishing. Anytime.

Little Jimmy used to fish a lot with Porter Waggoner, another huge Opry star. He says Porter is a great fisherman who taught him a whole lot about fishing. Mostly, Porter showed him how every artificial bait is different and needs to be used differently. Porter even sold Little Jimmy a boat once. Jimmy said he got a good deal!

Anyway, the day of our trip with Little Jimmy, we got in my truck and drove down to pick him up at his house in Brentwood, just outside of Nashville. We thought we were going to drive up in his driveway and wait for him. But when we came to his house, he was standing at the end of his driveway with his tackle box in one hand and his fishing rod in the other. Standing straight up and ready to go. We had to keep ourselves from cracking up because he is a dignified, older man. He's eighty years old. But he's a little guy, and it was really cute. He looked just as excited as the first time he ever went fishing. We were tickled to death to be going fishing with Little Jimmy Dickens, but he was tickled just to be going fishing. He was ready to go, wearing his baseball hat and flannel shirt. No rhinestones that day.

So Little Jimmy, Kelley, and I stopped and got ourselves some sausage biscuits, then we drove to Sand Mountain and had a blast. Kelley and I listened to stories like the one about how Jimmy went fishing once and broke his line. He told us how he loved to take his granddaughter April out fishing. He said it was such a thrill to watch her catch a fish. Then she discovered boys.

Little Jimmy also told Opry stories. He talked about Hank Williams. They were good friends. It's so interesting to me to be around someone who's eighty years old, knew Hank Williams, and played on the same stage with him. He watched country music form and evolve. In my eyes, Jimmie Rogers was first, but the person who formed country music as we know it was Hank Williams. He brought a steel guitar into it, and the arrangements were very similar to what we still use today. And this guy, Jimmy Dickens, was singing country music before anybody knew what country was.

Little Jimmy told another story during our drive to Alabama about how Hank Williams gave him his nickname, Tater. Years ago, Little Jimmy had a hit called "Take an Old Tater and Wait." One day, Hank walked in and said, "Hey, Tater!" And it stuck. To this day, that's what everybody calls Jimmy. The day I was asked to be a member of the Opry, when Jimmy walked out with Jeannie Sealy and Bill Anderson, he was dressed like a four-foot nine-inch Santa Claus. He said, "Brad, this is what you said you wanted for Christmas: Merry Christmas from Tater Claus." This was all on TV, which was pretty neat.

When we got out on the water, we didn't talk too much. That evening, we got real intense. I got one on, a bass that pulled the boat!

We were in a little john boat, and the bass turned the boat around. The fish never surfaced.

I ended up throwing the lure and not breaking the line. I'm very good about retying. I use good line and change my line. I pride myself on not breaking the line. If a bass is gonna come off, he's gonna throw the lure, and that's exactly what he did.

Every time I see Jimmy at the Opry, the first thing out of his mouth is, "I still have dreams about that fish." Just last weekend I saw him and he said, "I dreamt all last night about it. I don't think I slept."

A Fisherman Can Never Lose a Great Fish

The Florida Keys consists of a little spit of land that divides the Atlantic Ocean and the Gulf of Mexico. On either side of it, there is blue as far as you can see. It's a fisherman's paradise.

While driving through the Keys, travelers inevitably hit Islamorada, a tiny village located about halfway between Miami and Key West. It's difficult to miss Islamorada's famous beacon, Bud & Mary's Marina. The owner of the marina, Richard Stanczyk, is a man obsessed. Brad can relate to his obsession.

Richard Stanczyk is the definition of a fisherman. He is a guy who fishes for a living and fishes on his day off. He fishes every day. But you can't say he fishes for fun. It's too important to him.

The idea of going deep-sea fishing on a big boat never really appealed to me because I don't necessarily like any kind of fishing where somebody has to tell me everything to do. I don't like it when a

Richard Stanczyk in Islamorada, Florida

guy baits your hook for you, throws it in, and you just wait for your fish to bite. I like it better when I'm in control.

But I'm not against ocean fishing, per se. I love the idea of going after redfish or bonefish in the flats. I've done that in Corpus Christi. It was a blast. Certainly, every fisherman fantasizes about huge, jumping fish. We can all identify with the epic struggle—the Old Man and the Sea thing. That's intriguing.

Richard once had a struggle to match the famous one in Hemingway's book. To add more drama, he had to choose between the mighty fish and his favorite girl. Now, I can definitely relate.

It was forty years ago. The day of North Miami High's senior prom. Richard and his buddies planned to do it right. They all had dates and no curfew. What could be better?

Richard's date was Donna, his childhood sweetheart. She was a beautiful girl. A great catch. But the truth was, Richard wasn't as excited as everyone else about the whole prom thing. The only thing he seemed to get excited about was fishing.

He started fishing when he was three. His grandfather took him to a freshwater lake in St. Louis. He gave him a cane pole and a worm, and he fished between the cracks in the dock. Even with the equipment handicap, he managed to catch the fish of the day—a three-pound bass. He was hooked.

Later, his family moved to Miami and the ocean was his backyard. He couldn't have been more content.

Anyway, the day of the prom, he woke around eight to a great day. The perfect fishing day, that is. There was a light wind, blue sky. He only had to think about it a few seconds before deciding there was plenty of time to fish, come in early, and still get to the prom. His friends, Jeff and Tommy, were in agreement.

He called Donna, and she was not pleased. In fact, she thought he had taken complete leave of his senses. She threatened him with a fate worse than death if he wasn't home by noon.

The guys headed out about five miles, approaching the edge of the Gulf Stream. The water was deep purple, and there were patches of golden yellow weeds floating along the edge of a current line. It looked really good, and it was, for as soon as the baits hit the water, they were attacked by groups of large dolphin, big bulls with two more cows with them. They were biting like mad dogs. Soon, they had a boxful of fish. When things slowed down, Richard put out a different rig, a swimming mullet, hoping to get the attention of a sailfish.

Right away, something knocked down the bait. Richard locked up the reel and began to wind. There was something about this fish. It seemed really heavy and took off at speeds that made the line seem to melt off the reel. Richard's buddies turned the boat around as fast as they could to get behind the fish.

Finally, the fish settled down, and they began the fight. Luckily, Richard had a "fighting chair." (Actually, it was an old lawn chair with a gimble attached to it.) Thirty minutes went by, and they still hadn't seen this great fish. Nothing seemed to have any effect on it. They were at a standoff and being towed to the North. Richard was beginning to feel the strain of the battle. It was hot, and his fingers, back, and even his legs were tiring.

Richard describes the frustration and powerlessness he felt. His mind went back to the book he read in English class that year, Hemingway's *The Old Man and the Sea*. He said he loved that book. He found it hard to believe such a fish could exist, even though he knew they did. He wondered if he had found his Hemingway fish only six miles off the coast of Miami.

At noon, they had been fighting the fish for two hours. They were at least ten miles away from where they started. Then something changed.

The fish had been swimming steadily in one direction and what seemed to be one depth when suddenly Richard felt the speed pick up and the fish began to jolt hard and heavy, like a handshake.

Then, Richard heard Tommy and Jeff shouting and screaming. He turned and saw this huge fish exploding on the surface in a valiant series of jumps, which went on for hundreds of feet. It never went under; it just stayed on the top the whole time. They chased the line and finally caught up to him.

Three hours into the fight, Jeff broke the silence. "Think we should break the line?"

They were already past Fort Lauderdale and going north. Jeff pointed out that if they bailed now they could be home by three and still make the prom. Richard couldn't believe he was suggesting such a thing. Didn't he realize what this fish meant?

Richard said, "How about thirty more minutes?" They said OK, but now he had the pressure of the fish and the clock.

Just then, the fish rose up and broke the surface again, jumping in what seemed like slow motion. Only about half his body came out of the water, but the guys could tell this was an enormous creature. Richard's friends watched in awe. There was no more talk of giving up.

At that point, the sun was really taking its toll on Richard. He says he felt like the skin was burning right off his body. In those days, there was no sunscreen, but Jeff came to his aid. He had the great idea to spread peanut butter on Richard's face, lips, nose—even his ears. It helped, but the agony of the battle continued.

Six hours later, twenty miles up the coast and still heading north, and covered with peanut butter, things were looking bleak.

Richard also realized, when he landed the fish, they had no way to get him in the boat. This was the biggest blue Marlin he had ever seen. He thought when he caught him, surely the fish would die and they would tie him up with the anchor rope and tow him in, like Santiago did in *The Old Man and the Sea*.

After nearly seven hours, the sun was still pounding and Richard was exhausted. This was somewhere he had never been before—a mix of exhaustion and frustration. Think of the guy in the cartoon crawling through the desert looking for water. He was snapped back to consciousness when Tommy asked, "Hey, do we have enough fuel?"

They were thirty miles from home and in trouble. They had no water. They were out of peanut butter. They knew at this point, they could not make it home if they kept fighting the fish. They would end up in North Carolina or Europe if what they had heard about the Gulf Stream was true.

Richard decided to tighten the drag. The fish had to be as tired as he was. He took his fishing pliers and cranked down on the drag. It completely locked up. He held his breath as the line stopped going out.

Then, the great fish jumped one more time—twelve feet out of the water. Then he was gone. The line went limp. It had broken. There was something very surreal about it. Like a dream you couldn't wake up from.

Richard just slumped over in the chair and didn't speak or move for a long time. After a while he just started muttering. "We'll get another one. You'll see. It'll be even bigger."

Reality began to set in—the guys were nearly out of fuel. They were forty miles north of home and seven miles off the beach. They pointed the boat toward shore, hoping to find an inlet. Right at dark, they heard the sounds of the engine stuttering, starving for fuel, and finally, shutting off. They were adrift and out of fuel. Richard shut his eyes, picturing the marlin's final jump. Soon, he was asleep.

He woke to the sound of the boat bumping up against a seawall. They had drifted up to a beautiful home on the inland waterway. It was early evening and the lights were still on.

Since Richard still had peanut butter all over his face, he told Jeff to go knock on the door. The people were great. The guys gave them all the fish they caught.

Richard's dad came to pick them up. On the way home, Richard thought of Donna. He decided to tell her they ran out of fuel, drifted all day, and were finally rescued. He decided to leave out the part about the fish.

The guys had missed the prom. But they made it to the party afterward.

Richard says he eventually lost the girl—he remembers it being an honesty issue—but a fisherman can never lose a great fish. He never stopped chasing that blue marlin.

Lookin' for That One Percent

The musky, mostly found up north in Michigan, Wisconsin, Minnesota, and Canada, is arguably the most prized of trophy fish. Muskies are big, ferocious, and extremely hard to catch. Once Musky fishermen eventually land one, they tend to forget the thousands of casts that finally got them their "monster". One thing is for sure: they always have a great story to tell.

I've never gone musky fishing. At first, I was put off when I heard stories from guys who go musky fishing all the time and are tickled if they got one fish in a year! But they say it's awesome. So I'm keeping an open mind.

Joe Bucher is the founder of Joe Bucher Tackle Company. He also hosts the TV show *Fishing with Joe Bucher*. He says that if you're a good bass fisherman, you'd make a good musky fisherman. OK, I'm listening.

Joe knows about muskies. He's fished for them all his life out of his

Joe Bucher in Eagle River, Wisconsin

hometown of Eagle River, Wisconsin. He knows bass fishing too. He says the two kinds of fishing are a lot alike. According to Joe, musky fishing is just a larger version of bass fishing because you're using basically the same lures: spinner baits, crank baits, and jigs. The tackle is just bigger. Joe says anglers are using one of his baits, the Top Raider, in Gunnersville, Alabama, and getting huge bass!

Also, the techniques are similar. The only difference is with musky fishing, at the end of every retrieve, instead of pulling it out and firing another cast, you finish the retrieve with a figure 8, a movement where you trace a big, deep shape of the number eight in the water a couple of times. This gives muskies one more chance to hit the bait—they tend to follow it close to the surface, so you don't want to yank it out when the fish might still be there!

Joe says bass fishermen who want a bigger, toothier fish and a new challenge often come up north looking for muskies. They're big, strong, and powerful. You're talking about a fish that's thirty, forty, or even fifty pounds. But you'd better be patient. And if you're fishing with Joe, you'd better make a figure 8 on every retrieve, as if your life depended on it!

When he was working as a guide, Joe tried to teach the figure 8 deal to all his clients. Back in the mid-seventies, he was guiding two doctors at Big Lake, about twenty miles north of Eagle River. They were drifting across this weed bar, "Never Fail Bar," in the middle of the lake. (By the way, Joe says this bar failed him many times. He didn't name it!)

One of the doctors, a regular client, brought along a friend who was new to the sport. Joe was trying to go over the basics of musky fishing and show him how to figure 8, but he was one of these guys who talked a whole lot.

He was asking questions but didn't really seem to want to know the answers because before Joe could answer, he was already asking another question or answering it himself. That kind of thing. It was tough because with musky fishing, like bass fishing, concentration is important. Most guys want to keep it kind of quiet.

Joe kept telling this guy to figure 8 when he retrieved. He would turn toward Joe to ask a question, and he'd be holding the rod with one hand at the end of the handle. Not even with his fingers around the trigger portion of the handle. Joe said, "Man, you've got to figure 8 with both hands because if you don't, when a big fish hits . . ." Joe would tell him, and he'd hold on for one or two casts, then go back to holding on with one hand on the end of the handle of this big, two-handed casting-style musky rod.

So, they were drifting along. The doctor is talking away. Joe's in the back of the boat adjusting the trolling motor. All of the sudden he hears, "Ugh!"

Joe says, "What happened?" The doctor says, "The rod!" Joe says, "What rod?" He says, "Your rod! It's gone." Joe says, "What do you mean?" He says, "I don't know, but it's gone! I was doing one of those figure whatever things." Joe says, "Were you doing it with one hand?" He says, "I don't remember. I was too busy talking. But the rod's gone."

Joe figured that a fish struck. The doctor's talking on and on about how much the rod's going to cost and how he can't believe he dropped a rod overboard. Anyway, there wasn't very much wind on the lake and the water was fairly clear. So, Joe threw a floating marker out to hold the position where the rod went over and looked down in the water with his polarized sunglasses.

The funny thing was, the rod (these were pre-graphite days) was actually a Green Bay Packers rod, green with yellow wraps and a silver reel. So it was very visible. Joe sees a sparkle and a flash in the water— there it was! He was about to drop his lure down and hook the rod. Then, he saw a musky with a silver crankbait dogboned in his mouth! The rod was on top of a thirty-inch musky, who was just lying there on top of the weeds, with no clue what was going on!

Meanwhile, the doctor was talking with his buddy in the bow of the boat. Joe went over to the spot with the trolling motor and stuffed the rod down in the water, burying half his arm. He hooked the rod and got it up. Then the fish started tugging on it. But he's hooked on the rod and the line so he was fighting both. The guys came over to see what was going on. Joe handed his rod backward so he could get his hand on the other rod.

The doctor yelled, "That's my rod!" Joe said, "No! That's my rod!"

They ended up netting the fish—a thirty-inch musky. Then the guy really couldn't stop talking.

Last summer, Joe's son was up visiting before he went back to college. He brought his buddy from Alabama who had never fished for musky before. Joe was showing him this figure 8 thing. He kept shaking his head and saying, "I've never seen anything like this before! How am I doing?"

But he was doing it. Then, incredibly, the kid sees a musky following his lure near the surface. The thing is, Joe says if the lure is too close to the surface, the fish might see you and get spooked.

The kid yells, "He took off! He took off!"

Joe says, "Bury the rod!"

The kids says, "But he took off!"

Joe says it again, "Dangit! Bury the rod!"

This fish turned around like a bullet and just hammered it and came roaring out of the water. They got the whole thing on camera for Joe's TV show.

Beginner's luck. I like the sound of that.

I have to be careful not to get my hopes up like one of Joe's guests did. Not too long ago, Joe went to the Lake of the Woods in Canada to fish with the national sales manager for Flambeau tackle boxes. They had been up there for three days and hadn't even seen a fish. This guy had wanted to go musky fishing with Joe for years, but after three days of no action, he wanted out!

The tackle-box guy quit fishing after the third day. He was in the back of the boat sipping coffee telling Joe he was crazy. He said, "Cast, cast, cast, cast! You haven't seen a fish in three days. Don't you get sick of this?" Joe said, "Yeah! 99 percent of the time musky fishing stinks. But you know it's that 1 percent that I'm looking for."

There's an old saying, "When the wind's out of the east, fish bite the least." This had been true for them. The wind was out of the east for three days. And nothing. But then, the wind switched. All of the sudden, the front that had been there just blew out.

When the wind switched, Joe went to one of his favorite big fish spots. He told the tackle box guy, if they're going to bite, they're going to bite now! The guy just stayed in the back of the boat shaking his head. Joe heard him muttering, "These dang fish ain't worth fishing for."

The water was really turbulent. They could barely see the lake. Joe was bringing in the bait and doing his figure 8s, just like he'd been doing for the last three days. Then the guy asked him a question, something about flights out of Ontario. He still wanted to leave. So Joe was looking at him, figure 8ing. He looked down at the lure, then looked back at the guy. He was about to pick up the lure out of the water and make the next cast when this giant fish roars out of the water!

As he lifted the lure out of the water to make a cast, the musky followed it out of the water, engulfed it in midair, and splashed back into the water with the lure still in its mouth!

Now they had a green, wild, man-thrashing, thirty-five-pound fish on two feet of line, and he's jerking Joe right out of the boat. It was pulling hard. Then the fish fell back into the water and toppled Joe right off the deck. Joe was clinging with one hand to the gunnel of the boat. He had one leg hooked on the gunnel, too. The other part of his body was out of the boat. He was reaching out his left hand as far as he could, begrudgingly giving this fish a few inches of line. He had seventy-five-pound test line on, and the musky was peeling it off quick. It was mad, and Joe had nowhere to go but overboard with the fish!

Joe was just about overboard when the fish finally decided to back off. Then it turned around and went under the boat. Joe rolled back

Joe Bucher holding a muskie

into the boat and stuffed the rod down in the water so it didn't get caught on the edge of the boat and break off.

As Joe fought the fish, the tackle-box guy was yelling and swearing at the top of his lungs. He was saying, "You gotta do this! You gotta do that! This is unbelievable!"

When you hook a fish on that short of line, no matter what kind it is, it ends up burning out really fast. Joe says it's like standing in a ring going three rounds with Mike Tyson. Something's got to give! Joe's ribs were bruised. He says he felt like he'd been in a war with this fish. Finally, he netted it. A fifty-three incher! Thirty-five pounds!

I wouldn't have believed it, but Joe has it on tape. OK, Joe. You got me.

The Pressure Is On

Once an angler catches fishing fever, suddenly, what was supposed to be a relaxing activity turns into a hard-core sport. Then comes the urge to compete. That's what tournaments are for.

When I first moved to Nashville to attend Belmont University, I used to go fishing a lot with a buddy of mine, Brad Thompson. There were some great days out on the lake. I remember thinking that we were so good because we got to the point where, day after day, we were catching fish numbering in the teens. So we entered some tournaments. And it never failed—on tournament day, we never caught anything that was a keeper. No matter what. I mean, we could catch fish any other time!

Tournaments are fun, no question. But there's a lot more pressure. I enjoy participating in charity tournaments. Technically, there's less pressure than a straight-ahead competition because you're out there for a good cause and it's supposed to be fun. But I guess most guys can't help it. We still want to win.

My friend Tim Owens and I have gone to a few tournaments together. Tim's a songwriter, we work together a lot, but here's another guy who'd rather be fishing. But he's got it straight—he'd rather be fishing for fun. He knows how intense tournament fishing can be. He tried making a living at it when he still lived in Wheatland, Oklahoma, but he said turning fishing into work took all the fun out of it.

Anyway, in April 2002, Tim and I were fishing together in a tournament I hosted in Nashville, the Hook, Line & Singer Tournament to benefit St. Jude's Hospital. We got out on the lake, and I threw out a crankbait that got caught up in a tree hanging out over the water. It was really high up in the tree. I guess I wasn't paying enough attention. Actually, I was on my cell phone doing some radio interviews. I put my phone down, climbed way out on the front of the boat, and reached out to grab a limb of this tree. Tim was holding the boat steady to keep it from going out from under me. I couldn't get to the tree from the bank because it was so far out over the water. I was hanging from the limb trying to get my bait. I couldn't lose it because I'd already caught fish on it. I wanted to be able to keep throwing and catch fish.

Tim yelled, "You're going to kill yourself and drown over a three dollar bait!"

I said, "No. I just don't want to lose."

My good friend and fellow country singer Andy Griggs was one of the celebrity competitors at the tournament. He got in his boat around ten that morning (the weigh-in wasn't until about three), and got busy right away. Immediately, he hooked a fish that he said felt like a log! He stood on the edge of the boat and got ready to set the hook. But he wasn't holding the rod very tightly, and this fish, a nice one, ripped the rod right out of his hands and went into the water.

Since this was a tournament, a competition, Andy had no intention of letting that rod go. He watched the rod sink down into the water and without hesitation, just dove in head first!

He grabbed his rod and tried to throw it back up into the boat and get somebody else to catch the fish. Well, unfortunately they lost the fish. Andy climbed back in the boat. His clothes were dripping wet. Boats with TV cameras and spectators were all around. But Andy decided he wasn't going to spend another five hours sopping wet. So, he just took his wet clothes off—in front of everybody—and fished the rest of the day in his boxers.

There's a man who takes his fishing seriously. Even when he looks ridiculous.

That reminds me of another story about Barry Dodson, one of the regular panelists on the Fox TV show *NASCAR This Morning*. He's worked with lots of drivers, but his claim to fame was being Rusty Wallace's crew chief the year he won the Winston Cup. He'd rather be fishing, though. He participates in as many tournaments as he can.

A couple of years back, he got up around 5:30 in the morning and headed down to Lake Norman, near his house in North Carolina, to register for a tournament. He had been on that particular dock many times, so even though it was pitch dark, he just kind of felt his way to the water's edge and started walking up the dock.

Well, the dock was gone. He kept walking, right into the water. It was like seventeen degrees outside, and before he was even wet, he was covered with ice. Just iced over! Unlike Andy, he couldn't just strip off his clothes and keep going. He had to go home and change. But what struck him as funny was the fact that no one even looked up from what they were doing. Certainly no one stopped to help him. The other anglers just kept getting ready for the tournament. They never broke their focus, even to look at a guy covered with ice.

Every year there's a big tournament after the NASCAR race in Richmond, the NASCAR Invitational Bass Tournament. It seems like there is a ton of overlap between motor sports and fishing. Just like country music and fishing. And motor sports and country music.

Anyway, it's a big event, hosted by Woo Daves, a Bass Masters Classic champion. Many of the big NASCAR stars participate, and there are a whole lot of bragging rights that go along with winning!

Back in '95, Barry had had a really rough year. He suffered a huge tragedy when he lost two of his kids in a car accident. And he'd had a pretty rocky year racing-wise. Kyle Petty was his driver, and things had not gone well. So all Barry had to look forward to was this tournament. He really wanted to win.

They finished up at the racetrack Saturday night and went to bed around two in the morning—then got up around four for the tournament.

Everyone was paired up with a local guide. Barry and his guy headed out. It was a really windy day. Barry had his old fifteen-dollar Zebco 33, and his guide was fishing with crankbaits, really throwing them fast through the water. He asked Barry if he wanted to try a baitcaster, and Barry said no. I think he just wanted to use what he was used to.

The guide kept telling Barry he wasn't going to do any good with the gear he was using. "You've got to burn it through!" he said. "The ratio, the speed's not quick enough on that reel. You've got to burn it! Burn it! Burn it!"

Barry would throw it. The guide would say burn it. His arm was getting tired. So, when the guide wasn't looking, Barry just fished like he normally did. Even though his fifteen-dollar reel probably wouldn't bring back the bait fast enough to catch the fish. Or so the guide said.

By 11:00 A.M., Barry had his limit of five fish. And they didn't have to go in until three. He won with twelve pounds and thirteen ounces on four fish.

There was some hilarious ribbing and plenty of disbelief back at the dock. Some of the drivers, Bobby Labonte, Donnie Allison, and Tony Stewart teased Barry about his expensive gear. But don't you bet there was a run on Zebco 33s that weekend?

Always on My Mind

When you see a fisherman looking off into the distance, deep in thought, it's a no-brainer. If the guy had a cartoon bubble over his head we would see him standing on the bow of his boat with his rod bent over. Fishing is never far from his mind.

My songwriter buddy Tim Owens loves to tell a story about a concert we did last year in Montgomery, Alabama. It was Riverfront Stages, one of the biggest shows we'd ever played. They had big, drive-in-movie-type screens for people who weren't close to the stage. There were thousands of people, and they were going nuts. Coming up to the stage, throwing flowers, taking pictures.

I kept looking over at Tim, who was grinning ear to ear. When I came off the stage and headed down this huge ramp, I walked over to him and said, "You know what I was thinking?" He looked at me, all excited. "What?"

Brad Paisley in Nashville, Tennessee

I said, "If we'd gone up on the dam that morning and thrown Carolina rigs, we would've caught bigger fish."

He looked a little disappointed. I don't know. I think he thought I was going to say something about the crowd or tell him something profound like, "I'll remember this moment forever." But the truth was, I was thinking about fishing. That's true most of the time.

A few years back, before I had my record deal, I used to go down to my friend (and now producer and cowriter) Frank Rogers's beach house in South Carolina. We would go down there and write with Chris DuBois. Several of the songs we wrote, "Me Neither," "Who Needs Pictures," and a few others ended up on my albums. We wouldn't be there long before I'd take a break and head down to the water. Frank would laugh at me because no sooner would I get near the water than I'd have a line out.

He always says, "If Brad's anywhere close to water and can put a pole in, he will. Whether he's catching fish or not."

I guess he's right. When I do things like that people always ask, "Oh, are you going fishing to get an idea for a song?" The thing is, I hardly ever think about songs when I'm fishing. The point is to think of nothing.

Come to think of it, that's what I caught in the surf outside Frank's house. Nothing. At least I don't remember any bites. But another time, before a show in Panama City, Florida, I wandered out to the surf. There was this other guy fishing there too. He was using McDonald's straws as his "fly." I thought he was nuts. He cut the straws with a treble hook and put a weight on it. Then he threw it in the surf, and it would look like a darting fish. Like a fly!

I couldn't believe it. But he was catching sharks. So I did it and caught one too. A small sand shark.

You just never know. But that's the way I am. If there's water of any kind, I'm going to drop a line in it. If I had a swimming pool, I'd probably use it to test lures. Come to think of it, that would work great. You could watch the action.

I'm always looking for a place to escape to. A place to fish even for a little while. There's a little pond behind my house—that was one of the selling points for me when I bought the place. (The other selling point was that the garage was big enough to fit my boat.)

I've been trying to stock my pond. I've been bringing back blue gill from other lakes and putting them in there. I keep transplanting, but bass-wise, the pond just hasn't taken hold. It's sort of overrun with carp, which aren't ideal, but they're kind of fun to catch. I was thinking of bringing some kids out here to help.

Brad with two carp on one arrow

One thing I tried was bow-hunting for carp. That's a sport in itself! It's actually fun as can be. The first time my dad came to visit, shortly after I moved into my house, I brought him down to my pond and said, "Hey, watch this!" Boom! I got two on one arrow. I didn't even mean to. They were just stacked up.

The carp swim on the surface at certain times of the day. You just sort of zero in and shoot one. If you hit it, the arrow has a reel and line on it. You let them run a minute. Then you reel them in.

We've joked about having a carp-off! It would be a tournament where I'd invite as many people as I could and tell them, "OK, if you catch them, you have to keep them!" We'll have to see if we can get them out of there. Because they're probably not going to let the bass take hold.

I'm having trouble keeping bass in my pond. But my friend George Jones has bass in his catfish pond. Sometimes, I go over to his property and fish. He'll come down and see me when I'm there, but he doesn't wet a line. Fishing is more work than he's willing to do these days!

The funny thing is, he swears there's no bass in his catfish pond. But I do catch bass in there! He says, "There ain't bass in there. We didn't stock bass in there! Go to the other pond."

But the bigger ones are in the catfish pond. I don't know how they got there, but they ended up in that pond somehow. It must have overflowed or something. It's funny, because I'll tell him I caught a bass in there, but he doesn't believe it! I'll say, "I didn't?" He says, "No. You didn't because there's no bass in there." There's no way to prove it to him because I always release them back into the pond. So I just say, "OK."

You know, I want him to let me keep coming over. To catch those bass.

"The Grass Is Always Greener"

Fans of country singers, NASCAR drivers, or movie stars would probably be surprised to find out that even though it appears the stars they so admire are in possession of a dream job, secretly they dream of doing something else. Something even better.

My friend Tracy Byrd and I have a lot in common. We're both working as singers. We've both had some success at it. But both of us have a secret ambition: to fish for a living.

It was Tracy's dream to fish the trail and become a professional bass fisherman. He thought that was more realistic than becoming a country singer. He loved bass fishing so much, he figured that's what he wanted to do for his career. He fished tournaments for a while, but now Tracy says he's glad he ended up in the music business because it's an easier life than the grind of a pro bass fisherman.

Of course, we travel a lot in the music business. But those fishing guys travel hard. Many of them stay in campers, or if they're lucky, motel rooms, after fishing hard all day long. But the guys who have their own shows, now that's a different story.

Both Tracy and I fantasize about having our own fishing show. The big difference between us is that Tracy has gotten close to doing it. He was the sportscaster, the anchor guy of all the weekend shows on TNN Outdoors for three years before the programming changed. He went on to host Mossy Oak's *Hunting the Country* show, so he's in the ballpark. I know he'll have his own fishing show someday. He's a great storyteller.

Another thing we have in common is our heroes. We both idolize the guys we grew up watching fish on TV. Tracy says he was more excited to meet his fishing heroes than he was his music idols. I feel the same way.

Tracy says Bill Dance was the person he was most excited to meet. And now he and Bill have a lasting friendship. Once, a female pro bass angler told Tracy he reminded her of a young Bill Dance. He says he's never been paid a higher compliment. "Bill Dance is a step above everybody else," Tracy says. "He's just a great man."

When Tracy met Bill, of course he wanted to be invited to be one of

Tracy Byrd with Bill Dance

his on-air guests. But Bill is pretty particular. He and Tracy went fishing four different times before they even talked about doing anything for a show.

Several times Bill, who lives just outside of Memphis, found out Tracy was playing in Tunica, Mississippi. He called and said, "How about I meet you at I-47 and I-10 and we'll go fishing." Tracy always said yes, even if Bill wanted to meet early in the morning after a late-night concert. They had some great trips, but Tracy couldn't help but wonder if Bill was ever going to ask him to tape an episode.

Finally, Bill called Tracy and asked him to meet him in Florida to film a show. It just so happened Tracy had some tour dates in Florida, but he says he would have made it happen no matter what. Their destination: the phosphate pits just northeast of Tampa.

They fished for two days, and even though a cold front blew in, this spot where they fished was pretty much a sure thing. It was one of the many pits—there are probably 250 of them in that area—where companies mine for phosphates. The pits, anywhere from five to five hundred acres, naturally fill up with water. They've got fish in them, too, but they are seldom fished because they are on private property. Bill knows the folks who own them, so it's a great place to film a show.

Even with the bad weather—it was only forty-five degrees—they were catching fish, tons of tilapia perch, left and right. On the second day, they were sitting there, fishing in that cold, when Tracy looked way across to the end of the pit and said, "Bill, is that a naked man over there?"

Bill thought Tracy was kidding. But Tracy was serious. He said he swore he saw a naked guy at the end of the pit throwing a cast net. Bill said he must be seeing things because there's never anybody out there. It's private property, and they patrol it.

Tracy told him they must not be patrolling it very well because there was a naked guy out there, thigh-deep in the water, throwing a cast net.

So they cranked up the engine and took off. When they got closer, Bill said, "I'll be danged— that is a naked guy! That's a naked Mexican is what that is."

Then the guy saw them coming. He started trying to run, and he fell down in the water trying to grab his cast net, which was full of perch. As Tracy puts it, he was as naked as the day he was born! He tried to scoop up the fish and grab all his clothes. In the meantime, some other guys in a beat-up white van drove up with the door wide open. He dove in and they sped away.

The best part is, the cameras were rolling and they zoomed in on the guy! Bill has it on tape. I can understand these guys just trying to get some fish to eat. But I don't get the naked part. Tracy said it was freezing.

Maybe the next time I'm fishing alone in a phosphate pit I'll try it. Or, maybe not.

On Ice

Hard-core fishermen know no pain. Rain? They love it! Stifling heat? Bring it on! Cold? Not a problem. In fact, to thousands of anglers who live "Up North," where lakes freeze in the winter, cold is necessary because ice is what they're after. Ice fishermen are a breed all to themselves.

I've always been intrigued by ice fishing. Guys from the north who grew up drilling holes in the ice and dragging up perch and walleye swear it's the greatest thing going. And people who have never ice fished love to make fun of it. I mean, it does sound kind of crazy to sit outside all day in the freezing weather next to a hole in the ice. But I'd be willing to try it.

Probably the most famous place for ice fishing is Minnesota, where every winter, the thousands of lakes around the state are covered with semi-permanent huts like the ones in the movie *Grumpy Old Men*.

One of the best known ice fishing lakes is Mille Lacs, just north of Minneapolis. The lake is huge. Every year, as soon as the freeze hits, fishermen start hauling their shacks onto the lake. There are as many as five thousand out there some years! It's really a small town all it's own with unwritten rules and regulations such as, "Don't set up your shack too close to mine" or "Don't bang on my door to borrow bait unless you bring me some sandwiches."

Evidently, ice shacks have come a long way from the makeshift shanties they once were. One of the most impressive huts belongs to Kent Hrbek, who was a star first baseman and awesome hitter for the Minnesota Twins. Kent retired in 1996, and his first thought was: Mille Lacs.

You can't really call Kent's shack a *shack*. He calls it a fish house, and this place is nicer than some guys' apartments. He's got more stuff than I had in my first condo! Kent has a stereo (he says you've got to have tunes), a working satellite dish, two bunks, kitchen stuff, and a bathroom. Well, it's just a little room with a bucket, but it's impressive nonetheless. And of course, there's Kent's big old recliner where he sits and jigs for walleyes through one of the six holes in his "floor".

Kent spends much of the winter in his shack. He even sleeps out there—once he stayed for a three-day stretch. He doesn't miss fish when he sleeps either. He has this neat makeshift alarm hooked up to his tip-ups, the little contraptions that spring up ("tip up") above the ice when a fish sets the hook way down below. When the alarm goes off, Kent gets out of his chair or bunk and reels it in.

Kent has brought lots of friends to fish with him in his fish house. He grew up in Minnesota, so he forgets how people react when they first see heavy trucks riding across the ice on the way to these houses set up smack in the middle of the lake!

He laughs when he remembers the first time his friend Gary Gaetti came out to Mille Lacs with him. Gary is from Centralia, Illinois, so Kent thought he would have seen this kind of thing before. But it seems he wasn't too familiar with ice fishing because when Kent was driving along and turned onto a plowed portion of the lake to cut across and get to the other side, Gary's eyes went wide.

Kent never even slowed down, it was like he was on a regular old road. Gary was white as a ghost looking out the window going, "Are we on the . . . lake?" Kent says it always tickles him when he brings out first-timers.

He always hates it when February 28th rolls around. That's the day the shacks have to come off the lake. Then he has to wait for spring to go after fish in a plain old boat.

The Final Frontier

Every fisherman has the same fantasy of catching fish hand-over-fist in a pristine lake or river he has all to himself. There is a place where this fantasy can be reality: Alaska. But anglers lucky enough to venture to the Final Frontier need to beware. Even if you have the lake to yourself, you're never completely alone.

Alaska is the place I can't wait to go. I definitely want to know what it's like to land a big salmon, but I really look forward to being away from civilization. I want to get a sense of what this place was like before we settled it. In my mind's eye, that's what Alaska will be like.

There is one thing everyone equates with fishing and Alaska: bears. It's inevitable you're going to see one if you spend any time there. I'm kind of looking forward to it.

A photographer I know, Ron Modra, said he felt just the same way the first time he went to Alaska. He figured that everybody else deals with the bears, so if he saw one, he'd deal with it too.

Ron worked for *Sports Illustrated* for a long time, so he got to meet some great characters. One of the classic guys he got to know was John Riggins,

John Riggins, Ron Modra, and guide in King Salmon, Alaska

the Washington Redskins star. A while back, "Riggo" surprised Ron and took him on a trip to Alaska for his fortieth birthday.

They flew in on a little float plane to Mike Cusack's Lodge in King Salmon, Alaska. The lodge is an exclusive, awesome spot in the middle of nowhere. There is only room for about twenty guests—in fact, Ernest and Julio Gallo were there that same week.

The first day, they fished close to the lodge on the Naknek River. They were so happy about the twenty-four hours of daylight in the summer. They figured they could fish all night and just about did. Around two in the morning (they'd been out for a good sixteen hours), the guide begged for mercy, and they went in. Back at the lodge, either Ernest or Julio Gallo, Ron can't remember which, asked them if they saw any bears. Ron laughed and said, "Oh, they're afraid of us. They stayed away!"

The next day, they took the plane back into the Brooks Range to fish for sockeye salmon. As they were flying in, Ron looked down and saw his first bear. In fact, he saw a couple of bears. They were little brown dots making their way down to the river to fish.

Feeling a little tentative, they got out of the plane and waded into the river. Almost immediately, a grizzly appeared by the bank. She was so quiet they didn't notice her at first. Riggo had a fish on, and the guide calmly told him to snap his line. Riggo's eyes were as wide as saucers. He instantly complied. The rule was, let the bear have it. The last thing they wanted was for the bears to start making the connection between humans and fish—their food.

King Salmon, Alaska

They went upstream a ways. There they encountered even more bears. Ron says it was incredibly unnerving—they were only about twenty yards away—but he still felt fortunate to see these awesome creatures up close. Luckily, the bears were pretty intense about their fishing and mostly ignored them.

Later, on the boat, Ron and Riggo were giving each other a hard time. Ron kept saying stuff like, "Big, bad running back. Scared of a cuddly teddy bear. Wimp!" When they reached the dock, Riggo got his revenge.

Ron, who is about 160 pounds with rocks in his pockets, was standing at the end of the dock with his back turned. Riggo, who was about 245 pounds at the time, got in a three-point stance and hollered at Ron, "Hey! Who you calling a wimp?" Ron saw the MVP of Superbowl XVII charging at him full bore. He hit Ron in the chest, and they both flew into the water. It was freezing cold. Ron's waders were whipped off his legs and went flying down the river in the heavy current. It was moving really fast.

Then Riggo remembered: Ron can't swim. He grabbed him in a bear hug muttering, "Sorry! Sorry!" and threw him up on the dock. They both lay there, sopping wet, laughing hysterically. The guide just shook his head.

It's scary out there in the wilderness.

Fred Telleen has every angler's dream job. He has his own guide service, Mystic Waters, on the Kenai River in Alaska. After years of living in Alaska, his wife finally convinced him to spend winters in Colorado, where the sun actually comes out. But when spring comes, Fred returns to the Kenai and takes people on dream trips in search of rainbow trout, Dolly Varden, and of course, Alaska's prize: sockeye, silver, and mighty king salmon.

Fred has encountered his share of bears. It's a way of life for people living in Alaska. Although most Alaskans don't exactly look forward to

Kenai River, Alaska

stumbling into a bear, most have learned to live with them. The thing is, there's something they find much scarier: people.

A few years ago, Fred was guiding a group of guys out for sockeye salmon. It was late June, and they were using fly rods, which they had never used before! Two out of the three guys picked it up right away and caught their limit of three sockeyes the first day. But one of the guys just couldn't get it. He kept losing fish or snagging them in the back. Things just weren't happening for him.

The next day they went out again. He took one cast, and there's this huge commotion in the water. He shouted, "I got one! I got one!" Fred ran over with the net.

They drag it in, and it turns out that he had hooked a stringer of three sockeyes—three freshly caught fish somebody else had lost up the river.

The guy leaned back in his chair and said, "Well, I got my limit. I'm done!" He sat in the boat the rest of the morning waiting for his buddies to catch their limit. He didn't ever actually catch one of his own! But he was happy!

During one of Fred's earlier years guiding, he was scheduled to take two guys out together. They didn't know each other. One of the guys introduced himself by saying, "I'm from West Yellowstone, and I know how to fly fish."

Fred said, "That's great." He could tell by the guy's top-notch, but worn-out equipment that he had spent a lot of time fishing.

The other guy shows up and he's Mr. I've-just-been-to-the-Orvis-Fly-Fishing-School-and-I-don't-know-a-thing. That's why he hired a guide. He's totally clueless. He recently saw the movie, *A River Runs Through It,* and he's excited. He wants to go fly fishing.

So Fred headed out with his two clients, Mr. Experienced and Mr. Complete Novice. They got out on the water, and Mr. West Yellowstone started making these perfect sixty-foot casts. He would let his line drift for about three feet and make another big cast. Fred told him, "That's really great, but we're not fishing grasshoppers along the bank like you do on the Yellowstone. We're trying to imitate a salmon egg that's drifting along the bottom. Because the king salmon are spawning now."

But the guy from West Yellowstone just couldn't handle it. Every time he saw a big rock or a log or something, he'd cast into it. And he wouldn't let his line drift for more than a few feet before he'd pick it up and cast it again. But the bumbler, who couldn't cast to save his life, kept trying. It took heroic effort to move his line at all! But a couple of times, he managed to land it in a puddle just outside the boat, then boom! He had a five-pound rainbow on the line! It went on like that all day long.

Fred gently reminded Mr. West Yellowstone, the reason Joe over here is catching all these fish is because he's going where the fish are. You've got to let your line drift naturally with the boat and get your egg down to the bottom, so the fish think it's a real egg. But he couldn't handle it. He just had to make these long casts. By the end of the day the bumbler was starting to apologize! He was catching more fish and bigger fish.

The one guy had no skill but did what was necessary to catch fish on that given day. The other guy had skills, but he couldn't transition from his home water condition. He couldn't adjust. And even in Alaska, where the fish are everywhere, isn't that what it's all about?

Boys Will Be Boys

Country music stars spend a lot of time on the road. They often team up with other acts as part of a big traveling show, such as the huge George Strait tour in the summer of 2001. Brad was part of the line-up at this show. So was the mega-group Lonestar. Everyone got to know one another extremely well as they rolled their caravan into the next town, performing night after night.

These tours are a blast, but for the performers, they get somewhat repetitive. Boredom sets in. And trouble follows.

We were out with Lonestar on the George Strait tour last year. They followed my set, and we got into sort of a practical joke war. So they had a girl backstage talking to me through the monitor mix (through my headphones) trying to get me to mess up. I made it through without laughing or cracking a grin, and I thought that was all they were gonna do.

Brad Paisley in Branson, Missouri

So when I started singing "I'm Gonna Miss Her," my guard was down. Richie McDonald and Keech Rainwater, Lonestar's lead singer and drummer, were in the front row throwing minnows at my forehead. But the worst part was, unknown to me, they filled my water bottle with minnows.

I drank out of it twice while I was playing. The third time I went to take a swig, I looked down and saw them swimming around in there. I didn't swallow one, but the water definitely had a fish taste. I started cracking up and spitting it out at the same time.

I got them back, though. During that same show I closed my set with "Amazed," Lonestar's biggest hit. Sort of stole their thunder. So I got them back. If anything, I held my own.

Jokes aren't just an on-stage phenomenon. Guys, being guys, like to joke around when we're out fishing too. In fact, it's mandatory.

They take their joking pretty seriously in the Florida Keys. In fact, it's kind of scary. Richard Stanczyk, the guy who owns Bud & Mary's

Marina in Islamorada, told me about the time he met two guys from the Florida Marlins.

Doug Rader, (aka "Rooster") who was the pitching coach, and Bob McClure, a pitcher, came down to fish with Richard for the first time back in 1996, the year before the Marlins won the World Series. Today, Richard, Doug, and Mac are really good friends, but the first time they came down to fish with him, Richard was kind of on his toes. He wasn't intimidated, really. He takes lots of famous people out fishing. But that year everybody in Florida was talking about the Marlins, and these guys expected to catch a bunch of fish and still get to their game that night on time.

So they fished for a while. Then Richard, checking the position of the sun (he doesn't wear a watch), decided they needed to head back. He started racing back from the bonefish flats. He found himself in a channel on Snake Creek when two huge boats passed.

He was in a little seventeen-foot boat going fifty miles per hour, and he hit a complete rogue set of waves. Doug weighs 240 pounds, and he's holding a thousand-dollar fly rod in his hands. All Richard saw was Doug coming out of his chair and going backward right out of the boat. It scared him to death. He thought, "Oh my God, I've killed the Florida Marlins' coach!" He was stunned.

As time ticked away, Richard started panicking. Mac was asking, "Where is he? Where is he?"

Two minutes went by. It felt like forever. Richard kept thinking, "I've killed the Marlins' coach. And he's got my thousand-dollar fly rod, which is now in two pieces. What am I going to do?"

Finally, Doug hits the surface. He was laughing hysterically. He had actually exhaled before he hit the water, gone down fourteen feet, and sat on the bottom. He's a diver! Richard didn't know that. But he wouldn't forget it.

Oh, yeah. The Marlins won that night.

Disappearing acts are popular in the Keys. One of Richard's friends, Captain Jimmy Albright, was to fishing what Ted Williams was to base-ball. That's what Richard says, anyway. In fact, Jimmy and Ted were good friends.

Evidently, as Jimmy got older he became quite a prankster. And for a while he had a young protégé, who is now an old man, named Billy Knowles. One night, Billy took an angler out and anchored up in the sound. It was dark and they were mullet fishing for tarpon. Well, after a while, Billy fell asleep.

From way across the channel, Jimmy saw him and quietly pulled his boat up alongside theirs. Then he silently motioned for the angler to climb into his boat. Well, when Billy woke up, there's no angler in his boat. He was just horrified. He searched feverishly in the dark with his light, figuring the guy fell over. There was nothing for him to do but race back to the marina for help.

When he got there, the angler and Jimmy were sipping a beer.

And I thought the minnows were bad.

Before he became a country singer, my buddy Darryl Worley worked as a commercial fisherman. He did it to help pay his way through college. (He has degrees in chemistry and biology, by the way). He worked on the Tennessee River in the Pickwick Dam area, mostly going for catfish, but during the right time of year they'd go for spoonbill or buffalo fish.

Darryl also loves to fish for fun. And he always has fun when he fishes. He says what he learned about fishing is that the best-laid plans always seem to go awry.

Before he made his way to Nashville, Darryl worked in the chemical industry. For a time, he worked as a technical marketing specialist in Baton Rouge, Louisiana. He was trying to get some business from a paper mill in Saint Francisville. He knew there were a lot of guys who worked there that loved to fish. So, hoping to stir up some good will, he took some people from the mill out on a fishing trip down to the saltwater marshes.

There were six people on the trip, including the big boss man and some people who worked for him. The boss man also brought his father on the trip. On Darryl's boat, which was about fifteen feet long, there were three people fishing. That's close quarters when you're casting— you have to be really careful.

Anyway, after everybody got a bunch of redfish, they decided to head down the marsh a ways and go after some speckled trout. Right away, they ran into a huge school. Everyone started casting like crazy to catch as many as they could while the fish were feeding. The fishing was just great!

So Darryl was sitting on the boat in between the boss man and the boss's dad. He felt like he was stuck in the worst spot. Everyone else was just whipping their lures and dragging them in, while he was having to be really cautious. He had to take it slow just to keep from hooking anybody. At that point, Darryl says he remembers he had cast twenty-one times and caught nineteen fish! They were just piling them in the boat. That's kind of the way you have to do things. Get them while they're there. They tend to shut down pretty quickly.

So, on Darryl's twenty-second cast (his Catch-22, he says), he put his lure behind his back. His pole was up and he was in ready-to-cast position. He looked to his left to be sure the boss man was sitting down and out of the way. He looked to his right to be sure the man's father was sitting down and out of the way. Just before he cast, he

glanced down to his left and just hurled it. When he did he was looking straight ahead.

Then he heard the line pop. He looked over to the right and saw
that he had buried this big spoon lure in the back of the big boss man's
father's head. Not only that, he had snapped the line and almost jerked
him into the marsh!

Well, this poor guy has a treble hook buried in his scalp! What do
you do? Darryl said to himself, "Ohmagod!" It's one thing to hook the
boss man, but to hook his dad!

The dad was an older gentleman and a bit of a character anyway. So
he was a pretty good sport. Nobody freaked out. Darryl said, "OK, I've
been hooked twice. The best thing to do is to try to push that hook on
through and break the barb off, then you can pull it right out."

The boss man's dad said to give it a try. At that point, he said it
wasn't even hurting. So, Darryl gets in there and pushes and wrenches
on the hook trying to get it to come through the skin. He figured when
it made its way through, then they could cut off the barb. But the skin
on his head was just so tough! The hook would not come out. It just
bent the hook straight.

Finally, the boss man's dad said it was starting to hurt. So, they had
to drive back to town, all the way from Golden Meadow, which is deep
in the Louisiana Bayou. That ended the fishing trip.

Throwing out
One More Line . . .

Fishing is a whole lot more than a guy on a boat holding a pole with a string attached and waiting for a fish to bite whatever is dangling on the end of it. Fishing occupies your mind. In that sense it's the greatest therapy. Fishing gets you outside. In that sense, it's the greatest thing you can do to feed your soul. Fishing is something you do with people you love. In that sense, it's the best thing there is.

Photo Credits

Photo on pages 2, 4, 11, 32, 68, 70, 100, 115, 117 & 122 by Ron Modra

Photos on pages 22 & 114 courtesy of Ron Modra

Photos on pages 58 & 106 courtesy of Tracy Byrd

Photos on pages 14, 45 & 47 by Tony Phipps

Photos on pages 23, 50 & 102 courtesy of Doug Paisley

Photos on page 38 courtesy of Dawn Wells

Photos on pages 62 & 65 courtesy of Jimmy Houston

Photo on page 78 courtesy of Richard Stanczyk

Photos on pages 86 & 92 courtesy of Joe Bucher